I. Winslow Ayer

The Great North-Western Conspiracy in all its Startling Details

I. Winslow Ayer

The Great North-Western Conspiracy in all its Startling Details

ISBN/EAN: 9783337033118

Printed in Europe, USA, Canada, Australia, Japan

Cover: Foto ©ninafisch / pixelio.de

More available books at **www.hansebooks.com**

ORTH-WESTERN CONSPIRACY

IN ALL ITS

STARTLING DETAILS.

*c Plot to plunder and burn Chicago—Release of all Rebel prisoners—
Seizure of arsenals—Raids from Canada—Plot to burn New York
—Piracy on the Lakes—Parts for the Sons of Liberty
—Trial of Chicago conspirators—Inside views
of the Temples of the Sons of Liberty
—Names of prominent
members.*

ILLUSTRATED WITH PORTRAITS OF LEADING CHARACTERS, ETC., ETC.

By I. WINSLOW AYER, M. D.

FOR SALE BY
N R. WALSH, BALDWIN & BAMFORD, CHICAGO, AND ALL BOOKSELLERS AND PERIODICAL
DEALERS IN EVERY CITY AND TOWN IN THE UNION.

Entered according to Act of Congress, in the year 1865, by
I. WINSLOW AYER, M.D.,
In the Clerk's Office of the District Court of the United States, for the Northern District of Illinois.

CHICAGO:
ROUNDS & JAMES, BOOK AND JOB PRINTERS, ELECTROTYPERS AND BINDERS, 46 STATE STREET.
1865.

I. WINSLOW AYER, M.D.

INTRODUCTION.

The trial before the Military Commission in Cincinnati, just concluded, was in many respects one of the most remarkable events of the war. The investigation has elicited testimony of the most startling character, showing conclusively to the minds of all reasonable men who have given to it careful, earnest attention that there was a most formidable, deep and well arranged conspiracy, which, but for timely discovery and judicious action, would have resulted most disastrously, not only to the particular cities and towns specified and doomed to destruction, but to the whole country. None can contemplate the danger through which we have passed without a shudder and without a recognition of the hand of a merciful Providence who has guided our beloved country in its darkest hours and who has crowned our struggles for liberty and union with glorious victory.

To have proclaimed to the public, even a few short months ago, that a scheme had been concocted in Richmond, of so vast and formidable a character, so insiduous in its operations, so complete in its details that it had found favor and support in all the great cities and towns in Illinois, Indiana, Missouri, Kentucky, Ohio, Iowa, and sections of other States that scarcely a village was exempt from its corruption, that it numbered in its ranks more traitors in the aggregate than the number of brave men in the combined armies of the gallant Grant and Sherman, and that all who had thus united recognised but one common cause—the destruction of our country, the defeat and humiliation of our people, and the triumph of the Rebellion—the author of such a proclamation would have been written down a madman or a fool, by most persons in the community; and yet the developments before the military tribunal have established the fact, to the eternal infamy of all who were leagued in the conspiracy.

As the trial opened, and the charges of the indictment were made public, all sympatisers with the conspiracy affected to disbelieve its existence, and raised their eyes and hands to Heaven, in pious horror, and prayed that *justice* might be meted out to the accused, who were, they claimed, the best of citizens, the most devout Christians, the most zealous patriots, the most earnest advocates of law and order, and that their accusers might be shunned of all good men forever. To this prayer the accused will scarce utter the response, Amen! Even some good, careful, honest Union men, astonished at the startling revelations, refused, for a time, to believe that there was any truth in the allegations against the prisoners; by degrees, however, as corroborative evidence accumulated, the truth was forced upon their minds, and there are now few persons of ordinary intelligence and candor, who have not been able to discover that "there was something in it, after all," and that we have been Providentially saved a most terrible disaster.

But the investigation has been lengthy, and the reports in the newspapers have been brief and irregular, and few, comparatively, there are who have heard or read all of even the more important testimony, or appreciate fully the vast magnitude of the conspiracy; and there are many who having read only the indictment, have conceived the idea that if the charges therein alleged are true, the crime was confined to a few desperate and wicked men in Chicago alone, and that, therefore, it possessed but a local interest. Such a conclusion is wholly groundless. The history of this conspiracy is of the most vital interest for the people of every State in the Union, for had the conspirators not been foiled at a most opportune moment, their plans would have been successful in every particular, and once in operation they could not have been frustrated by any force we could have arrayed against them; and who shall say that had the savage hordes of Jeff. Davis then been turned loose upon an unarmed community, to carry desolation and ruin as they should sweep over our fair States, that to-day the Southern rebels would be, as they now are, in their last extremity—that victory would now be perched upon our banners wherever our noble pioneers of freedom advance, and that our brave boys of the Potomac would now be reposing from their labors in the halls of the rebel capitol! Those who, upon investigation, fail to recognise the magnitude, the sagacity, the completeness of this Northwestern Conspiracy, and realise its immense importance to the rebel chieftains at the South, corroborated as the evidence before the Commission has been by incidents of almost daily occurrence for many months, have not learned to read correctly the history of the Great Southern Rebellion. If an idea ever entered the heads of malcontents at the North to establish a Northwestern Confederacy, it was speedily chased away by the more promising schemes of the arch traitor late of Richmond. It is to collect facts already elicited, and to give further information, and with a hope of aiding the cause of the Union so sacred and dear to us all, that the writer has yielded to the oft-repeated requests of his friends to present a connected and concise history of the Northwestern Conspiracy.

THE AUTHOR.

CHAP. I.

SECRET SERVICE TO SECURE SUCCESS OF SOUTHERN ARMS—STATE SOVEREIGNTY—THE GENERAL PURPOSES OF SECRET POLITICAL ORGANIZATIONS—RECOLLECTIONS THAT CAN NEVER DIE—VOICES FROM OUR BRAVE SOLDIERS AT THE FRONT, BESPEAKING OUR PROTECTION FOR THEIR WIVES, CHILDREN, PARENTS AND HOMES FROM NORTHERN COPPERHEADS—CHARACTER OF THE LEADERS OF THE DIFFERENT SECRET ORDERS.

The signal potency of secret organizations at the South prior to the secession of States, and indeed the only really effective machinery by which an attempt at disunion by the people could have been made to appear possible, early in the great struggle engaged the earnest attention of the Southern leaders. Knowing as they did that had the question of secession been primarily an open one, for free discussion, that the masses of the people would have rejected the proposition with deserved scorn and indignation, and hung the ambitious adventurers who dared propose the sacrilege. They realized the importance of establishing the order in the North. The leaders saw with delight the working of secret organizations, where men were sworn to secrecy, and drawn onward step by step, till they reached the very brink of the fearful precipice. Thus did the people fasten upon themselves and each other the shackles of slavery, which they have since so unwillingly worn. The doctrine of State sovereignty proclaimed by John C. Calhoun, and which, together with its apostles, Jackson well knew how to receive, had been instilled into the minds of the people of the States, which since their admission into the Union had been at war with destiny, and in the hope of securing perpetuity of their peculiar institutions, they attempted the disolution of the Union. Truly gratifying it must have been to the extremists in those States to have watched the gathering clouds, and to listen to the low murmuring thunder which pressaged the coming storm, and well they knew how fearful would be its fury, but blinded to the inevitable result, they were confident of ultimate success, when they should have so far disseminated the Calhoun poison at the North, as to have made oath—bound slaves in such numbers as would paralyze the efforts of Union men, and render it necessary to recall our armies from the field to suppress insurrection at home, and to change the theatre of the war to Northern soil. None knew the importance of introducing the machinery of secret political organizations better than Davis himself, for he had not forgotten the Charleston Convention, the working of the secret orders then, and subsequent events had of course confirmed him in the opinion that a divided North would not be a formidable adversary, and that he was warranted in the firm belief that his wish to be "let alone" would be realised. With these views, shrewd and sagacious men established themselves early in Missouri, Kentucky, Indiana, Illinois and other States, and put the machinery in motion. The order sprung up in various sections of the country, and treason flourished well, as poisonous plants often show the greatest vitality. This plan was a success. Men high in rank and station—men from every profession and walk in life, embraced the principles of the order, and soon it could boast of legislators, judges of the higher courts, clergymen, doctors, lawyers, merchants and men from every avocation. Judge Bullitt, from the Supreme bench in Kentucky, Judge Morris of the Circuit Court of Illinois, Judd and Robinson, lawyers and candidates for the highest State offices, Col. Walker, agent of the State of Indiana, editors of the daily press, and men high in official station, and in the confidence of the people, ex-Governors of States and disaffected politicians, all seized upon this new element of power and with various motives, the chief of which was self agrandisement at any cost, even at the cost of our National existence—entered with zeal upon the work of disseminating the doctrines, and extending the organization throughout the North and West.

The leaders gratified by success, courted the support of the organizations they fostered till the candidates for the highest offices in the State and Nation felt certain of obtaining election, were they but in favor with the secret orders they aided in establishing. While the leaders were men of cunning, many of them of intellect and education, the rank and file was made up of different material. It not being necessary by the tenets of the order that they should *think* at all, brains were at a discount—muscle only was required—beings who would fall into line at the word of command and follow on to an undertaking, however desperate and criminal, without asking or thinking, or caring for the purpose to be attained; beings who could be put in harness and led or driven wherever and whenever it might suit their masters. Men from the lowest walks of life were preferred. In the lower strata of the order, social distinction was waived by the leaders, and the lowest wretch in the order was placed on a level with judges, merchants and politicians, at least within the hall of meeting, thus offering inducements potent enough to make the lodge room a place of interest and pleasure, and thus the organization thrived.

It became known of course that secret organizations of a most dangerous class were in existence, and their fruits were easily recognized. Our brave boys in the army were often importuned by letters, to desert their posts and to betray their flag. Union men were subject to annoyances that became unendurable, soldiers wives and families were grossly insulted, soldiers visiting their homes upon furloughs were often assaulted or murdered, quarrels upon petty pretexts were incited, neighbors arrayed against each other, dwellings burned by incendiaries, unoffending union men murdered, military secrets of greatest importance betrayed, libels of the most gross and malicious character by such papers as the Chicago *Times*, and by such men as Wilbur F. Story, its editor, till at length a voice came to us from the army in the field, which was often echoed, begging Union citizens at home, by their love of the Union, by the love they bore their own families, to protect the absent soldiers' wives, mothers, sisters and firesides from the Copperheads who remained at home; they would meet the enemy at the front, they would march fearlessly to the cannon's belching throat, and meet death or mutilation upon the field of battle for their Country's cause; not for themselves did they know fear or care for danger, but when the tidings came to them from home, when after toilsome marches, hunger and fatigue, or suffering from wounds received in desperate engagements, when resting a brief hour, and their eyes fell upon missives from home, from wives who bade them go and fight for freedom, and return not with shame upon their brows, when tender thoughts of home, of children and every "loved spot" that they had left behind, came crowding to their minds, who shall say that they were wanting in heroism if their faces became pale, their lips trembled and the tears dimmed their eyes, as they read of wrongs and insults endured from Copperheads at home, or of plots and acts by cowardly traitors to aid the common enemy; and when their entreaty comes to us to strike down the deadly foe at home and give protection to the helpless, let him blush with shame to call himself a man, let him never claim to be an American citizen, never claim protection of our Country's flag, let him close his ears to the sound of rejoicing for final and complete victory, let him only hold companionship with cowards and with culprits, and hide himself from the light of day who will turn a deaf ear to the soldiers' prayer. Copperheads who have withheld their sympathy and their efforts for our country in its days of darkness and of peril, should and will be known of men in all future time; their lives will be blighted, their names will be a reproach and a by-word, their children will blush for their parents, and the name of Benedict Arnold will no longer be the synonym of treason and betrayal—*his* name will be rescued from the infamy each passing year of the existence of our country has heaped upon it, and the Copperheads of the present day will receive the anathemas of all coming generations, till their very names shall be a curse too horrid for mortals to apply, and thenceforth be only echoed in the lowest depths of hell.

By Providential discovery of the existence of the Order of Sons of Liberty in Chicago, and the utmost vigilance, prudence, perseverence, patience, promptness and daring, the aims, designs and acts of this Order, of the American Knights and kindred organizations have been brought to light, its every evil purpose and plan laid before the Government, and the pet institution of Jeff. Davis has been turned inside out, so that "he who runs may read;" the curtain has been raised and the light of noonday has been let in, discovering to the public the horrid creation of traitors in our very midst—people who breathe the very air we do, who enjoy the same blessings and privileges, aye, and perhaps sit at the same tables. The friends and sympathizers of these traitors have sought to cast obloquy and distrust upon the statements of those who have successfully broken up the great conspiracy, and perjury has sought to blacken their reputations, but in vain. *Truth will prevail.*

The list of names of the members of the Sons of Liberty have been obtained and preserved, and will be valuable for reference hereafter.

As the reader passes down South Clark street, at the corner of Monroe, he will notice upon the right a large building of peculiar structure, and now bearing the name "Invincible Club Hall." It was here the temples of the Sons of Liberty, or, as they were then called, the "American Knights," held their secret sessions, going stealthily up the stairs singly or in groupes of two or three, to avoid observation, and when once inside the hall they were guarded by an outside sentinel, whose duty it was to apprise them of danger and to guard against its approach to the "temple"; but let not the fault-finding Sons blame their tyler now for any neglect of duty; once under the ban of suspicion he has proved himself as staunch a rebel and traitor as Jeff. Davis himself, and is entitled to all the consideration of a "devilish good fellow." But within a year, more or less, the "temple" of the *Illini*, as it was called, removed from Clark street to the large building upon the corner of Randolph and Dearborn streets, known as "McCormick's Block." Every Thursday evening prior to the eighth of November 1864, the windows of the hall in the fifth story gave evidence that the hall was occupied, but further than this evidence was not for the observer, however curious he might be, unless, perchance, he was a member of "the Order." Clambering up the long flights of stairs that lead to the hall, on a Thursday evening, the party in quest of discovery would be not a little surprised at the class of men he would notice upon the march upward; he would involuntarily button up his pockets and keep as far distant from his fellow travelers as possible, for a more God-forsaken looking class of vagabonds never before entered a respectable building, and it is a matter of some doubt whether so many graceless scoundrels were ever before convened in one building in Chicago, not excepting the Armory when the police have been unusually active and vigilant. Occasionally a fine looking man would brush hastily by you, as if afraid to be discovered and recognised—not in the least conscience-stricken, perhaps, for his purposes and intentions. Should the gas-light show to you the comely features of the Grand Senior Obadiah Jackson, Jr. Esq., on his pilgrimage upward, you would scarcely be willing to believe that he was the presiding genius of the room in the upper regions, and bound to dispense light and wisdom to the motley crowd who would so soon be filling the hall with fumes of cheap tobacco and the poorest quality of whiskey, mingled with the fragrance of onions, borne by gentle zephyrs from yonder open vestibule. Yonder comes L. A. Doolittle, Esq., a lawyer of some distinction and a justice of the peace; he wears a look of wisdom, and you can read upon his face that he is certain that the "despot Lincoln," and "Lincoln's hirelings," and "Lincoln's bastiles" are all going under together beneath the wheels of the triumphal car drawn by the opposition party, with Vallandigham as the leader. But we will not try to find any great number of fine looking men in very close proximity to the hall. Arriving on the fifth floor, and proceeding to a door upon which you find the sign of the "American Protestant Association," your friends casting furtive glances around and behind them, disappear by the door and are lost to view; one by one, like stars upon the approach of dawn, our constellation vanishes. You open the door, but your curiosity is not repaid; the seedy friends who preceded you but an instant are lost to sight—presto! the room is as vacant as a last year's robin's nest, and observation detects a hole of six inches in diameter in a door in one side of the room; you try the door, but it is fast, and you may leave if you wish, but the idea of a Copperhead crawling through a hole six inches in diameter will haunt your dreams that night.

CHAP. II.

FOREIGN POWERS THE ENEMIES OF REPUBLICAN GOVERNMENT—
THEIR PART IN THE PROGRAMME OF THE REBELLION.

The event of the American revolution burst upon the world as the most startling era in the history of nations. Monarchical Europe had long envied the proud career and inevitable destiny of these States, which had been shaken as the brightest jewels from the British Crown. Monarchs, Emperors, Queens, lords, princes and diplomats, who wield the sceptre of dominion, could not conceal the joy afforded them by a scene, which executed, promised the speedy extinguishment of the leading national power on the globe, and the final demolition of the only altar of liberty upon which the fires of freedom had continued bright.

The event created the more joy, because it was attributable partly to the efforts so strenuously put forth for many preceding years by the combined enemies of American Independence, to poison the American mind and breed disunion in the ranks of a free, industrious and honest yeomanry, with a view to the ultimate dissolution of the bonds of the Union.

These enemies, however, for some time anterior to the development of the fruit of their labors, had begun to despair of the cause in which they had engaged, and it is possible that the scheme of American wreck and ruin upon their part had been permanently abandoned, hence their immediate demonstrations of joy at the triumph of their cause of sedition.

But seeds sown, however barren the soil, seldom fail of some growth, and subsequent to the presidential election of 1860, the great American rebellion became transparent to both friend and foe. To enumerate and examine in detail the different phases of the programme of artificial causes which precipitated defiance of the General Government, and gave origin to the chronic disorder of the people of different sections upon the subject of their government, would occupy more space than has been allotted this brief narrative, which is more especially intended to embrace a readable compilation of the later movements of the enemies of the Government to crown the Confederate cause with success, through the bloody implement of Conspiracy and Revolution in the Northern States.

Having alluded to the prominent part occupied by foreign hostile powers in the general scheme of Conspiracy against the Federal Government, a brief allusion to the part executed by the native born American will not be out of place.

The cheek tingles with the blush of shame, when alas, it *must* be said that the pride of the American has been humbled by his too faithful adherence to the grand original compact of treason, even after the second most potent auxiliary to the plan had been tenderly touched with the wickedness of the scheme, and had withdrawn in dismay at the approach of the enactment of crime so revolting.

All things material and tangible have their bases and starting points, so too, had the Southern Rebellion its foundation stone laid deep and solid in the minds of the people by John C. Calhoun, the first great Supreme Commander of the germ from whence sprung the various elements of treason, which have entered into the composition of the powers seeking the destruction of the Federal Government. As for the doctrine of State Rights as expounded by Calhoun, it is carried beyond the Virginia and Kentucky resolutions of '98, to that point which renders it destructive of the end for which it is claimed to be enunciated.

It has been sought to carry the doctrine to that extremity beyond the exercise of its own reserved powers, which must inevitably bring it in collision with the legitimate operation of the powers delegated to the General Government.

With this extreme, hence fallacious, doctrine of State Rights thus firmly imbedded in the hearts and heads of a zealous people, rendering them, upon conscientious principles, the ready tools of ambitious leaders, filled with lust for power and place, it should not be a matter of so much surprise, that, after years of uninterrupted and persistent education and training of the generations in their order, that the year of 1860 found the continent trembling beneath the crack of musketry, the tread of horse, and the roar of cannon.

As among the more important means used by designing men in aid of the scheme of rebellion, and the ultimate establishment of a separate government in the South, the nucleus of which was to be the cotton states, secret organizations, assuming different names and traditions in different localities in the South were established, having for their special mission in the meantime the privacy of the plot, and the education of the people to that indispensable standard of treason which would eventually lead them to avow their principles at the point of the sword.

These organizations, in point of antiquity, are traced to a time not long anterior to the nullification of South Carolina in 1832, which was so promptly suppressed by General Jackson, then President of the United States. Some of them, however, claim even greater antiquity, and point with affected pride to the historical period of the American colonial revolution against the taxation and tyranny of England, as the date of their origin. Whatever may be the facts as to the precise date of the existence, respectively, of these disreputable cables, laid to undermine the greatness and glory of the National Union, cemented as it is by the blood of the sires and sages of the Revolution, is unimportant to the purpose of the author, while the great living fact that they have been the most deadly weapon in the hands of the enemy is corroborated by the eventful history of the union of these States.

Prior to the breaking out of the rebellion in 1861, these various organizations, being the van-guards in the general conspiracy against the integrity and perpetuity of the Federal Government, had not been introduced, to any great extent, in the non-slaveholding states, and in consequence thereof had little or no tangibility north of the compromise of 1820, familiarly known as Mason and Dixon's line. South of this line, however, they had long been standing institutions in every city, town, hamlet, villa and populated district throughout all of the late so-called Confederate States of America; vieing the Palmetto in rankness of growth, and rivaling the rattlesnake in deadness of poison, until at length, gorged with their own baneful offspring, and pale with the sickness of their own stomachs, the child of secession was born unto them as a curse and reproach to the Southern people and the generations to follow them forever.

On the 17th of April, 1861, the report of the gun fired upon Fort Sumpter was heard by every member of these secret conclaves in the South, and was the signal for the opening of the outer gates of every temple of treason in the land.

From that inauspicious moment forward to the present, no mask has hid from the scorn of the Christian world treason's hideous visage, but that blear-eyed monster, armed with every weapon of iniquity which devilish invention could devise, has alternately, with rage and despair, rushed to and fro across the continent, spilling the blood of innocence.

When, upon the occurrence of the Presidential election in 1860, it was found that the kernel planted by Calhoun had been fostered to maturity by secret organization, the blood and treasure of seven states was at once staked upon the fearful result, and the disruption of the Republic and the erection of a slave-driving despotism upon the ruins solemnly declared. In the outset, it was thought by leading political minds at the North, that but little sincerity could be attached to the assertion of independence by the Southern people. But as time elapsed and the contest grew more formidable and bloody, Northern men began by degrees to comprehend the magnitude of a chronic conspiracy which had cost the life-long labors of its ablest advocates to prepare. And though the hosts enlisted in the execution of this conspiracy for a time won the prestige of victors upon fields of blood, knowledge of their sincerity of purpose and the extent of their carefully collected resources at length came to every loyal man in the country, and vigorous measures, corresponding to the necessity, were at once devised, the effects of which are now seen in the capture of Richmond and the surrender of Lee.

Earlier than this date in the progress of the struggle, however, it became manifest that the wheel of fortune would eventually turn against the cause of the

South in consequence of her comparative weakness to contend against a power so amply provided with the material of war as the government at Washington. Then it was that the project of enlarging the area of the rebellion, first fell upon the Southern mind as indispensable to their cause, now fast becoming desperate in the extreme. Hurried raids into border northern states gave to the prowess of southern arms but momentary *eclat*, and little or no enduring strength was added to the stability of the Richmond government, beyond the plunder obtained in the line of march. On the contrary, these raids, instead of being evidence of the power of the South to maintain the standard of independence, were looked upon by the military chieftains of the North, without apprehension further than the demoralization, consequent upon the particular neighborhoods and districts thus invaded. In fact each recurring raid gave additional grounds for the confident belief on the part of the North, that the downfall of the rebellion was but a question of time, much sooner to be solved than many people of both sections supposed. These symptoms of the distress of the cause meantime did not escape the sagacity of the leaders of the rebellion, and as an expedient remedy, the plan of secretly organizing traitors in the northern states was determined upon as early as 1862, by the political representatives and agents of the confederate states, the attempt, character and success of which project will be the subject of the next chapter.

CHAP. III.

ARENA OF THE REBELLION EXTENDED—SECRET ORGANIZATION—PLAN OF FORMATION—KNIGHTS OF GOLDEN CIRCLE—TRANSPORTS ON THE RIVERS BURNED—EDUCATIONAL PURPOSES—SUPREME COUNCIL IN NEW YORK—DEGREES OF THE ORDERS.

As above intimated, early in 1862 the Richmond Government foresaw the necessity of bringing to its aid the hitherto comparatively dormant resources of treason in the Northern States, and the enlargement of the arena of the Rebellion. Raids having ominously failed in their design to arouse the lethargic spirits of Northern sympathizers and advocates, to rush to the standard of the misguided South, it was immediately determined to prolong the war, at least, to the date of the next Presidential election, and then through the agencies of secret organization and equipment, seize upon the excitement of the people in a hotly contested election, to force a rebellion against the administration elect in the North, as had been done in the South in 1860.

The executive part of this object was at once given into the hands of such trustworthy men, both North and South, as were deemed suitable to the enterprise, and the work of secret political organization was vigorously begun in Northern Missouri and Kentucky, from thence it gradually spread, until it was firmly rooted in the political tenets of the minority party in the States of Illinois, Iowa, Indiana, Ohio, New York, and portions of other adjoining States.

Much dissimilarity existed in the operative structure and formation of the various organizations, from time to time thus instituted. To give the public a full and complete description of these organizations, would be foreign to the writer's time, space and purpose, but in order that some record of their character may be made, a general description of each in its order in point of time, with a reference to the features in which radical dissimilarities appear, would seem indispensible to the poor perfection sought to be obtained by the author of these sketches.

Upon the discovery by Southern leaders that their cause must fail unless "fire in the rear" was at once instigated in the North, the Order of the Knights of the Golden Circle, an old Southern institution, was infused with life, and began its pilgrimage Northward, one additional creed having been ingrafted upon it.

It will be remembered that this Order was originally composed of the wealthiest planters, merchants and professional men of the South, and had for its sole object the inculcation of treason against the United States. It was simply an institution to educate the Southern mind to the required standard of rebellion. But when the Order was introduced into the North, it was found feasible to give it a double capacity, first that of an educational capacity, and second that of an incendiary capacity, which comprised the destruction of government property, and the houses and property of leading loyal citizens of the North, known to be strong advocates of the suppression of the rebellion. But this organization in name and cardinal purpose was short-lived, its career having subserved but a meagre benefit to the South, in a practical point of view. The damage it did was principally confined to the burning of United States transports on the Ohio and Mississippi rivers, and the moulding of the crude opinions of its members, which served as a solid foundation for the establishment of the Order of American Knights, which immediately succeeded its dissolution.

Like all institutions of iniquity, the sun of the Order of Knights of the Golden Circle went down in blood, but was the signal for the advent of an Order better calculated to meet the ends of its design.

It had been seen upon experiment that the Golden Circle had been successful beyond the most sanguine expectations of its instigators, and as the necessity of Northern revolution to insure the certain success of the Confederacy daily became more apparent to the rebels, both North and South, the Order of the American Knights was inaugurated—the executioner of that fell purpose. Its sun arose to its meridian with the suddenness of a meteor, doomed to flash across the canopy and burst in scattering atoms.

The Order of American Knights was erected upon the dissolved fragments of the Order of the Knights of the Golden Circle, which Order, in name, was abandoned for the additional reason that the suspicions of the Government had begun to be aroused as to the character of its movements. At the time of the extinction of the Golden Circle, its members were at once inducted into the Order of American Knights, so that this Order obtained much primary advantage, in point of numerical strength, over its predecessor, for the Golden Circle had already insiduously crept into the very hearts of several Northern cities and states. The American Knights being composed in the outset wholly of men who from experience had discovered whatever defectiveness may have been chargeable upon the Golden Circle, it was sought in the new Order to remedy the evils of the old Order.

With this in view, looking over the former and later phases of the Golden Circle as it had existed in the North and South, respectively, it was agreed to give the new Order still another capacity, and what was called the military branch or department was added, the incendiary capacity of the old Order being merged into this new military department.

We have seen that there had been in the North an Order mainly of educational capacity, contemplating revolution so soon as the public mind could be put in readiness for such an event, but now for the first time we find an Order prepared in its organic structure, to speedily collect together the elements of revolution and set them in motion. Such a concern was the Order of American Knights. True, the rise of the Order created a momentary excitement in political circles, as yet unaccustomed to dealing with the stern problems of Northern revolution by resort to arms. But, by the admirable adjustment of the administrative powers of the Order, into degrees, sub-degrees and departments of degrees and sub-degrees, the leaders were enabled to give to each adventurer in quest of the hidden mysteries of the so-called impartial maxims of genuine Democracy—that Democracy which *boasts of having permeated through every fibre and artery of our political, commercial and social systems*, a comfortable and genial sphere in which he was left to operate upon his good behavior.

Upon this ingenious plan the vast body and mass of the Order simply held the relation of probationary membership, until they were rendered competent through the educational capacity of the society, to advance into full fellowship with its diabolical design. A glance at this organization will suffice to show the shrewdness of the transient and local agents of the Confederacy, in their formation of an Order, having for its mission the attainment of so many incidental objects, without in the meantime subjecting themselves to the dangers of collision in their machinery. Accordingly, the Order was composed of three general degrees, viz.: First, the Temple Degree, second, the Grand Council Degree, and third, the Supreme Council Degree.

The first or Temple Degree, resembled the county organization of a State, and held the same relation to the second or Grand Council Degree (which was the state organization of the Order,) that our county government holds to our State government, and it was always sought to establish this first or Temple Degree at each county seat in a State, as expeditiously as possible, that the second or Grand Council Degree could the sooner be fully represented, and begin its State management of the Order. In other chapters the writer has made a passing, though sufficient allusion to the internal workings of these Temples, and doubtless the initiated reader, in different sections, will recognize the facts we have already and are further about to state, notwithstanding the "*obligation*" the author is supposed to have subscribed to, not to reveal the existence of the Order and its secrets, under *penalty of "suffering a shameful death."*

The process usually followed in instituting the Temple Degree, was to send missionaries with authority, into the districts proposed to be organized, who called together such of the "unterrified" leaders as were known to be "*sound* on Jeff. Davis' goose," before whom the design and object of the Order was confidentially laid for their approval or rejection, by a majority vote. It is important to recollect that the record does not afford an instance where a majority of those assembled for this purpose, rejected the Order as inconsistent with their political views. On

THE MILITARY COMMISSION IN SESSION IN THE ROTUNDA OF THE COURT HOUSE IN CINCINNATI.

"All whom we arrested wore the same general wolfish aspect."—From the testimony of Brig. Gen. B. J. Sweet.

the contrary, it was everywhere received by the politicians, both great and small, as "*just the thing they had been looking for.*" These politicians were then left to "manage their own local affairs" concerning the Order, "subject only to the constitution" of *Jeff. Davis.* Generally, several meetings and some discussion enabled these empyrics to determine plans of strategy to screen themselves, by "*covering the tracks in the sand,*" a remark frequently heard from members.

The plan in most cases adopted, was to familiarize a sufficient number of the *elect*, with a grossly immoral and treasonable pamphlet, called the "Ritual of the Order," to enable them to officer the Temple, and "induct" any number of "candidates" *supposed* to be "in waiting in the ante-room, into the sublime," but in fact dark and dubious "mysteries of the Order."

After one or more squads of these "candidates in" anxious and breathless "waiting" had been inducted, (meanwhile staring like stuck pigs at every object and officer which met their eyes,) in addition to the regular officers of the Temple already installed, it was considered that enough official and canvassing material had been acquired, and the more prominent politicians, not officers of the Temple, deemed it prudent to absent themselves from most of the weekly meetings. Again, it was an illusion of these leaders, to put forward the most irresponsible persons at their command, as the mouth-pieces and official representatives of the Order, to the end that if detected, the theory of *crazy, powerless fools*, could be wielded upon public sentiment by an undisturbed partisan press, to save the scheme from thorough investigation and development by the authorities.

In evidence of the fact of these illusions, L. A. Doolittle lectures the Temple in Chicago on the "purposes and plans of the Order," (but who by the way, was not so "insane on the subject" as the men who put him forward have sought to show him to be,) and prominent politicians, not before known to be members of the fraternity, appear prior to semi-annual elections as candidates for representatives in the Grand Council.

It was duly announced, also, that an extra session of the Supreme Council had been convened in the city of New York, charged with the special business of revising the ritual, changing the signs, passwords, grips, and giving to the Order a new name. Pursuant to announcement, Charles W. Patten made his appearance in the Temple with the rituals and paraphernalia of the new Order of the Sons of Liberty—the result of the proceedings of the late Supreme Council.

This obscure individual, with fame limited to the dusty walls of the Invincible Club Rooms and the traitor's dungeon at Camp Douglas, upon his appearance in the Temple, assigned two chief reasons for the recent action of the Supreme Council First and most important was, the obvious inadequacy of the Order of American Knights to subserve the purpose for which it was instituted, in consequence of the subordination of the military to the civil department. And, second, the disclosure in St. Louis had rendered the Order liable to intrusion by spies, an embarrassment to be avoided only by alteration of signs, grips, passwords, and name. We were then informed that we were Sons of Liberty (a sensible man would have said sons of the devil, if he had dared to have spoken the truth), and earnestly exhorted to exercise the utmost caution in adhering to the new rules and instructions of the Supreme Council. It is not a little amusing to witness the homœpathic doses of modern democracy, carefully administered to the rank and file of the northern people through the medium of these Orders.

In the first place, the Golden Circle edifies the "stranger advancing in dark, devious ways" with lessons upon the doctrine of state sovereignty, and admonishes him to "follow the straight and narrow path which is paved with gems and pearls, and bordered with perennial flowers whose perfumes all his senses will entrance," all of which is received by the sincere candidate with every mark of approval. We next find the American Knights embracing its members in the bedazzling folds of military lace to be used when in arms against the Government. A splendid spectacle of the doctrines of Washington, Jefferson, Jackson and Douglas! And to cap the miserable climax, men boasting of the Democracy of their fathers in a line of lineal descent for generations back, are required to subscribe to the doctrine of the subordination of the civil to the military authority by the tenets of the Sons of Liberty.

This astonishing feature of the Sons of Liberty, as contradistinguished from the Orders which preceded it, at first met with murmurs of disfavor, but the dissatisfaction was principally among men who ultimately acted the *nobler part*, and as the tide of treason rolled up to sustain this measure "for the good of the Order," all such were submerged and lost sight of, except by the evil eye set upon them as spies.

Without offering his advice, the writer would respectfully ask the *true* Democrat, who may yet, from the temptations of firmly-rooted prejudices, incline to the belief that this organization was purely democratic in the Andrew Jackson acceptation of that term, how the above statement of principles comports with his notions of the doctrines of the party with which he has hitherto seen fit to fellowship?

Is it not clearly to be seen that this Order meditated the establishment of a government more despotic in its character than history furnishes any example of? A government with three degrees or departments, each oath-bound and a profound secret to the other, moving in their appointed spheres, and the civil departments of which were secondary, in point of power, to the military departments!

Let no man, of whatever political persuasion he may be, flatter himself for a moment that such a government could be Republican in its nature.

Having now traced, with perhaps a tedious hand, the rise and fall of two political Orders, ranking among the most powerful instruments of crime and public wrong of their day, the writer bids their unmourned remains farewell, to pass to the consideration in the succeeding chapter, of the desperate career and final explosion of the Order of the Sons of Liberty—a solemn warning to the American people forever.

To save the Goudys, Caulfields, Adams, Edwards, Duncans, Wickershams, Cuttings, and Kimberlys, the Morrises, Walshes, Jacksons, Pattens, Gearys, and

Doolittles were put forward because they were eager for the fray, and possessed the temerity to brave the danger of Union bullets.

We have now seen how the Temple or First Degree was instituted in counties; how the various elements of treason were collected together and detailed for their special service of educating the ignorant, manufacturing materials and munitions of war, and devising plots to burn, plunder, and pillage unsuspecting cities; how each member was singled out according to his fitness for certain duties, which he performed without their character coming even to his fellow members of the same degree; and how the brained leaders of these institutions retired to the back ground to elude the vigilance of the ministers of the law, and "adjust the wires" that were to check to-day, and to-morrow precipitate the conspiracy.

The Grand Council, or Second Degree, was established in every State where the Temple Degree had obtained any strength and character as to numbers. This Degree resembled the State in its governmental organization, and bore the same relation to the Supreme Council or Third Degree that the State governments of the Federal Union bear to the government at Washington. The Order having a military department, these Grand Councils, in council assembled, adopted the militia and other statute laws of the particular State, with such revisions, exceptions and additional laws as were deemed essential to the successful operation of the Order.

Regular semi-annual meetings of the Grand Councils were held, convening respectively on the 22d of August and the 22d of February—the latter, in sacrilege be it said, being religiously observed as the birthday of Washington.

But extra sessions were almost monthly called during the year of 1864, prior to the election, to take precautionary and other expedient action upon the continually recurring changes of that eventful year. No considerable battle was fought in the front, that was not the signal for the assembling of this council, and no political event of any importance transpired that did not receive the solemn deliberations of this already *de facto* legislative body. Of course no person ever became a member of this Council who had not first been inducted into the Temple, and then by his Temple elected as a representative in the Grand Council, the election for which purpose was held semi-annually as above, and new representatives took their seats at each regular session.

The Grand Council embraced in its sphere of labors such duties as experience seemed to dictate, as being necessary to the fulfilment of the mission of the Order. It provided remedies for unmistakable evils, and watched with a zealous care and fostering hand, every interest of treason within the boundaries of its jurisdiction.

The Supreme Council or Third and highest Degree of the Order in organization, was built after the pattern of the Federal government at Washington, and wielded a similar general control over the affairs of the Order, that our National government exerts over the consequences growing out of the union of the States under one central government. Here we see how admirably the design to effect Northern rebellion was conceived. The whole machinery of a government *de facto*, and in disguise though it was, with all its branches, both civil and military in active operation for months and years within the very sound of the echoing steps of senators in the halls of the Capitol, was indeed a source of the most serious concern to the authorities, for the safety of the Republic. But valorous daring, tempered with prudence, was destined to bring to the light of day this infernal work of years, and accordingly the city of St. Louis was the scene of the first public development of the Order of American Knights, early in the spring of 1864, the principal facts of which disclosure the public learned from the press at the time, hence the writer will only allude in this connection to the effect created in various Circles of the Order, by the attempt upon the part of the Government to thwart the perpetration of the red-handed crimes contemplated by the leaders. When it was officially announced by Reuben Cassile, presiding Grand Seignior of the Chicago Temple, then recently removed from the Invincible Club Hall to McCormick's Building, that disclosures of the Order in St. Louis had occurred, every countenance was stamped with dismay. The timely appearance at the Temple, however, of Judge Morris and other leaders, served to interpose restraint upon any serious apprehensions of difficulty resulting to the Order.

CHAP. IV.

NEW ERA IN SECRET POLITICAL ORGANIZATIONS—PLEDGE TO "TAKE UP ARMS" FOR JEFF. DAVIS—TRUE DEMOCRACY STRUCK DOWN—NATIONAL AND STATE LEADERS—INVINCIBLE CLUB LEADERS—VALLANDIGHAM'S RETURN TO THE STATES IN HIS CAPACITY OF SUPREME COMMANDER OF THE SONS OF LIBERTY.

A new era in the history of secret political orders was opened by the Sons of Liberty.

As the Presidential election of 1864 approached, the party in the minority began to appreciate the awkwardness of its attitude upon the political issues of the day, and appeared determined in its conclusion to obtain the ascendency in the coming administration, by means of fraud and force.

The great mass of the party had now become conversant and familiar with every species of political crime, through secret organization, and it only remained for the leaders to decide upon a programme, to have it executed with despatch and fidelity.

Languishing under the lash of chastisement inflicted upon those infamous enough to aid and abet the cause of dismemberment, mutual hate and slaughter, National extinction and death, they swore in this Order an eternal and most dreadful oath of vengeance upon their offenders, and pledged themselves, under fearful penalties of death, " ever to take up arms in the cause of the oppressed in their own country, first of all, against any monarch, prince, potentate, power or government usurped, and found in arms and waging war against a people or peoples, who had of their own *free choice*, inaugurated a government for themselves, in accordance with and founded upon the eternal principles of truth."

Thus, the lovliest form of ancient or modern civilization, in a republic just rising to the glories of empire, was to be sacrificed to the mad notion of petty "State Sovereignty," by a sworn band of desperadoes. How sad when other generations would ask, where is the Federal Government, to be answered only by poets, who would sing her elegy, as in the past they have sang that of the lamented Hellas:

"Ask the Paynim slave,
Who treads all tearless on her hallowed grave;
Invoke the spirits of the past, and shed
The voice of your strong bidding on the dead!

> Lo! from a thousand crumbling tombs they rise—
> The great of old, the powerful and the wise!
> And a sad tale which none but they can tell,
> Falls on the mournful silence like a knell.
> Then mark yon lonely pilgrim bend and weep
> Above the mound where genius lies in sleep.
> And is this all? Alas! we turn in vain,
> And, turning, meet the self-same waste again—
> The same drear wilderness of stern decay;
> Its former pride, the phantom of a day;
> A song of summer-birds within a bower;
> A dream of beauty traced upon a flower;
> A lute whose master-chord has ceased to sound;
> A morning-star struck darkling to the ground."

The thought of the miserable commentary stirs the ire of the patriot and nerves his arm to daring deeds, in the holy cause of liberty, the constitution, and his country.

Skulk back into your dark dens of iniquity, you Clement L. Vallandigham, and you James A. McMaster, and you S. Corning Judd, and you Amos Green, and you P. C. Wright, (in Fort Lafayette where you ought to be,) before the wrath of honest people falls upon your wicked heads! Each of you, with the exception of *you*, Wright, being too infamous for that, even, have been before the Commission at Cincinnati, and stand before an outraged people condemned out of your own lips! Dare insult the light of day with your hideous faces, and be dashed in pieces on the rocks of public scorn!

But to return to our text, the Sons of Liberty, we find that undaunted organization in full blast from the time of its official inception in New York up to the Monday morning of the arrests on the 7th of November last.

It is now proposed to show, by an allusion to certain prominent facts occurring during the summer of '64, that the so-called Democratic party was the mainspring to the great conspiracy that has been attempted in the North with so much audacity that many men of the best judgment can scarcely believe it to be a reality. In this we do not wish to be understood that all men who have heretofore voted the "unterrified" ticket, have knowingly and willingly given aid and comfort to the treasonable plans and purposes of their leaders, for our personal acquaintance among that class of anti-administration men, is sufficient to enable us to say, with confidence, that many of them are as loyal at heart as any man who ever breathed the air of an American freeman.

But we mean this, and proclaim the fact in the face of every foe, that upon the death of that lamented statesman and patriot, Stephen A. Douglas, the Woods and McMasters of New York, the Seymours of Connecticut, the Vallandighams and Pendletons of Ohio, the Voorhees and Dodds of Indiana, the Judds and Greens of Illinois, and others of like ilk in other States, obtained the chieftainship of the party and inveigled its too pliable ranks into the prostituting embrace of this foul conspiracy, to overthrow the government and crown with success the cause of the confederate arms. It must be readily seen by every honest man of ordinary intelligence, that such an affair could never have gained a foothold among our people under a truly loyal condition of the opposing party. The truthfulness of this assertion is so very forcible to the candid reader, that illustration or argument in support of it would be superfluous. However, occasional incidents will serve better to connect popular leaders with the subject of these sketches, and call to the minds of participants practical facts.

Brig. Gen. Charles Walsh, some time during the winter of '64 and '65, received his quantum of a fund, of which we shall hereafter speak, to purchase arms to be distributed in the 1st Congressional district of Illinois, comprising the county of Cook, and the scene of the late Chicago conspiracy, the enactment of which was to be the signal for a general conflagration of our cities, and thus fulfil the prophecy of Jeff. Davis, that the grass would grow again, on the streets of the cities of the North.

Do the leaders of the Invincible Club, among whom are W. C. Goudy, John Garrick, Malcom McDonald, and Dr. Swayne Wickersham, remember that that institution was to be the public mouth-piece of the Sons of Liberty, in an address to the Democracy of Chicago, to have been issued during the Presidential campaign?

Do they also remember the joint delegation of Invincibles and Sons of Liberty that received Vallandigham and the Woods of New York, on their arrival in Chicago to participate in, and mould the proceedings of the National Democratic Convention?

Do they further remember the remarkable speech made in their Hall during the Convention, by Capt. Rynders of New York, whom they hissed from the platform for his bold and fearless expression of loyal sentiments?

Do they remember the motto, "Never worship the setting sun," which appeared on transparencies, and frequently fell from their own lips, and was meant as a hit upon those who were supposed to have allied themselves with treason, because of their belief in its eventual success?

Do they remember how it was proposed that Charles Walsh, of the Sons of Liberty, was to negotiate a purchase of the Chicago *Post*, and convert it to the same villainous purpose of its cotemporary, the *Times*?

Have they forgotten the fifty or sixty thousand dollars raised by subscription to the books of the Club, nominally to be used for procession and illuminating purposes, but which was used for the purchase of arms and the importation of butternuts, to engage in the attack upon Camp Douglas?

Have they forgotten that large sums of this money was obtained under false pretences—under pretences that it was to be used for ordinary campaign purposes?

Have they forgotten that through their instrumentality the McClellan Escorts, then organized in every ward, were officered by Sons of Liberty?

Have they forgotten the meeting of Invincible Club members and Sons of Liberty in the *sanctum sanctorum* of the Chicago *Times*, where the question of punishing Col. R. M. Hough and Mr. Eddy, in redress of personal injuries alleged to have been inflicted upon Wilbur F. Story, was gravely discussed by B. G. Caulfield, O. J. Rose, Alderman Barrett, S. Remington and others, and where also, large numbers of muskets and smaller arms were exhibited?

And lastly, have they forgotten that the Sons of Liberty, upon a certain occasion well known to every Copperhead member of the last Common Council of the city of Chicago, held themselves in readiness till after midnight, expecting to be called to the assistance of that, at that time, treasonable body?

None know the significance of these questions better than the persons above mentioned, and *others who were on hand about those times*. The merchants of South Water street in Chicago can now, perhaps, explain why they were called upon to subscribe so heavily to the books of the Invincible Club, and the writer would suggest the propriety of these merchants compelling those who solicited these subscriptions, to deliver up the arms so purchased, or refund the money to its rightful owners.

It is pretty well understood, we believe, that the Bridgeport Irish, vote the "*straight ticket.*" It is said, also, that James Geary, a Son of Liberty and "old clothes man" on the corner of Wells and Madison streets, could "influence hundreds of them by the wave of his hand." Now this "old clothes man" was empowered to furnish food, raiment and shelter to all escaped rebel prisoners, and charge the same to the Sons of Liberty, *alias* the Invincible Club, which, it is thought, *sometimes paid such bills* out of South Water street money *subscribed for processions and illuminations*. These facts are the keys to the revenue plan of the Sons of Liberty.

The complicity of the "*straight ticket*" voters in this scheme is further shown by the character of their State ticket, headed by Robinson for Governor, Judd for Lieut. Governor, and Hise of La Salle for Auditor, each Sons of Liberty, and Judd the Grand Commander of the State. If, as it would be made to appear, there was no complicity between the Democracy and the Confederate agents, why did Vallandigham, the Supreme Commander of an Order having its inception in Richmond, address the people from every stump in Illinois? If there was no complicity, why did Vallandigham, on his return from exile, in his official capacity, with his staff around him, defy the United States government that had justly banished him—with 80,000 Ohioans at his command?

If no complicity, why did all the rebels and confederate agents in Canada come to the Chicago Convention, and why were they here again at the November election? Copperheads of Chicago and elsewhere, answer these questions!

CHAP. V.

INSIDE VIEW OF A LODGE OF THE SONS OF LIBERTY IN CHICAGO—OPEN EXPRESSIONS OF TREASON—SIGNS OF THE TIMES—WAITING FOR REBEL VICTORIES—THE GREAT PEORIA PEACE MEETING—WHISKEY, TREASON AND GUNPOWDER.

Prior to July 1864, the information of the public or the authorities, in respect to the aims, intents and objects of the organized bands of home traitors, was very meagre and indefinite, for it was no easy task for detectives or loyal citizens to enter the portals of the Temples. True, enough had transpired at the investigations, and before military commissions in different sections of the country, to awaken a painful interest and unceasing vigilance on the part of loyal men. So well were these organizations guarded, that vigilance committees of their members were appointed with imperative instructions to report the names of all civic officers and detectives in the employment of the United States and Provost Marshals, and all persons, by whomsoever employed, who should attempt to obtain the secrets of the Order. So complete was the organization, that lists of names were reported and read at the weekly meetings, and the following day the names and descriptions of such officers were thoroughly circulated and reported to the brethren in other cities and towns, and as well might a belled cat hope to invade the precincts of rats and attain success, as for such a "spotted" individual to gain access to the Temples of American Knights and Sons of Liberty. Not a change was made on the police, not an increase or decrease of Provost guards, not a change of even the location of artillery in Camp Douglas, no change, however minute of interest to the rebels, was made but that it was reported and discussed within these nests and dens of treason.

It was atempted on several occasions by parties of loyal men, to ferret out and secure the secrets of the Order, but as well might an attempt have been made to possess the secrets of the Council of Ten, by the officers of the governments of Europe; it was almost impossible, and yet the developments upon the recent trials show conclusively, that had the task not been effected, the most terrible results would have ensued. With the desire to aid the Government to the extent of individual ability, it was not strange that when opportunity occurred, whereby all might be known, and that knowledge applied to the benefit of our bleeding country, that any loyal man would have availed himself of it, at any hazard. The writer found such opportunity, and waiving all personal considerations, undertook the task, trusting in God for success, and conscious that all good men would approve the motive, and that if for a time, reproach and calumny should cloud his reputation, or if perchance the assassin's hand should execute the sworn purpose of the Order, as the penalty for surrendering them to the hands of our Government, the time would surely come when the motives and the acts would find that approval in the hearts of all honest men, as it did in his own. Confiding the information accidentally obtained to W. H. Rand, Esq., of Chicago, a gentleman whose patriotism and whose reputation needs no encomiums, he immediately advised the expediency of conference with the State Executive, and to the honor of Governor Richard Yates, it should be said, he fully realized the importance of acquiring reliable information of the plots of the secret ally of Jeff. Davis. By Governor Yates an introduction was given to Brig.-Gen. Paine, then in command of the department, and again full and unqualified approval of the course thus far taken, was expressed, with the urgent request to follow up every avenue of information in this direction. Gen. Paine issued an introduction to Col. B. J. Sweet, whom he declared to be a "model man and a model officer in every respect," and in whom all confidence in so commendable a cause might be reposed. How nobly, how wisely and how well that gallant officer discharged his trust, all who have observed his course will concede, and that man whose heriosm at the memorable battle of Perryville, and on other battle fields, will ever be held in grateful remembrance by his countrymen, has added new lustre to his name, and the hearty benedictions which will ever be invoked for the defender of Chicago—the noble Col. Sweet—attest the satisfaction and joy of the people, to know that his services in this most difficult and hazardous undertaking are appreciated by the General Government, and the star upon his shoulder will glitter brighter as time wears on, and Copperheads live only in history, an evidence of how low men may sink in the scale of morality, and a warning to all future time.

For the writer to have hesitated in a course of duty so plain, and yet so distasteful, would have been criminal, cowardly, and unworthy of an American citizen. The advantage gained was followed up unremittingly, by day and by night, for many weary months, regardless of all professional duties and personal considerations. It was at the outset found highly necessary, if not indispensable, to have the concurrence of one good, loyal man of marked qualification—one who was discreet, who had experience upon police duties, who was prompt, energetic, persevering, patient, fearless, and withal a strictly honest man, a citizen whose reputation was above reproach; that man was found; he was Robert Alexander. After brief consideration, Mr. Alexander gave to the writer his hearty and earnest concurrence. Nothing was left undone by him that could further the hazardous undertaking, and personal gratitude for his ready acquiescence, which we tender to him, will meet with a ready response in the hearts of all good citizens.

It is now Thursday evening in July 1864. We will now ask the reader to go again with us up those long, tedious flights of stairs to the outer rooms of the "temple" of the Sons of Liberty in Chicago. We left the room before with the remembrance of only a hole six inches in diameter for a full sized Copperhead to crawl through, but we shall have better success this time. Advancing to the aforesaid door, and giving three distinct raps, the slide, which we find covers the hole from the inside, is moved up, and a live, full-grown Copperhead peers through the orifice. We whisper the word " Peace," or " Peoria," or whatever the monthly pass-word is, and the door is open, and we find ourselves within the vestibule of the temple, surrounded by a little group going through the preliminary exercises of initiation. We see the candidate and sponsors, with hands uplifted, and listen to the very poor reading of an officer, from the ritual, and giving the new comer his first dose of States' sovereignty and secession. This is so mystified and clouded with high-sounding words that the poor devil nods at every time the reader stops for breath, or to expectorate tobacco juice, and the ceremony is concluded, and the candidate, respectable for the good clothes which he wears this night as a rarity, follows his conductor to another door, where he hopes for admission, the only impression on the candidate being, that his right arm is weary from being elevated so long, and that he is coming rapidly into good fellowship with men of high judicial standing, who propose to give Abolitionists and Lincoln particular " hell under the shirt tail."

Again they knock and are challenged by an inside guardian, who lectures the newly fledged Son, who having nodded sufficiently, is conducted to the Ancient Brother in the West, so that the *Son*, reversing the order of nature, begins rising in the West. The " Ancient Brother " is a better reader, for here we find *brains* for the first time, as it is the leaders, as we have already said, who do all the thinking, unless, perchance, the simple wretches find themselves in Camp Douglas, where they begin thinking for themselves. While the Ancient Brother is reading to the attentive comer, now happy in the thought that he has taken himself in out of the *draft*, let us survey the sanctum sanctorum ; but first let us advance to the centre of the hall, where we find a piece of dirty oil cloth the size of a door mat, and stepping upon this, with body erect and turning our back upon the Ancient Brother, we find ourselves facing the Grand Seignior, who, on our first introduction, is Judge Morris; we salute, which we do by applying the palm of our right hand to the lips, then turning the hand to his seigniorship and bringing our left hand across the breast, which salutation being returned by the Grand Seignior, who sits upon a raised platform and wields a gavel, we take seats wherever our sense of cleanliness will permit, and where we hope there may be no traveling minute messengers conveying ideas from one man's head to another.

On the north side of the room is another platform and desk, where a guardian sits and addresses the candidate, who is supposed to lose his way and to be set right by this guardian, and even if the candidate is thoroughly sober he may be excused for losing his way, for it is a matter of much doubt whether he was ever in such a labarynth of words as he has just heard from the Ancient Brother, who, having given the man some pretty strong obligations, to endorse and support the policy of Jeff. Davis, together with an intimation that if he ever exposes any of the secrets, he may expect to suffer all sorts of penalties, and told him to fancy he had just received an acorn, the emblem of the order—he now sits down quietly in the pleasant consciousness that " we have got one more good voter on our side." The guardian of the North having put the new *Son* on his way, he appears in the East, reflecting his effulgence all around. The Grand Seignior now rises from his seat, drops his gavel and explains the mysteries of the initiation, giving him another dose of secession, about as much as the poor fellow can carry; tells him how to challenge a brother, concluding by giving the grand sign of distress, which is by raising the right hand and calling out *"Ocoon"* three times, which he says is made up of the name of *Calhoun*, whose name is mentioned with great reverence. Thus closes the ceremony of initiation. " Considerations for the good of. the Order" being the next order of business, speeches are made by some of the older heads to make the new one feel at home. This " feast of reason and flow of soul" over, other business is transacted, and the temple is closed, the Grand Seignor occasionally expressing a few words of caution, saying that but few members must be present at the meetings at *this* hall, as the presence of too great numbers will excite suspicion and lead to arrest. The next weekly meeting similar events occur, but *new faces* appear at every meeting, that is to say, the greater number of members who were present last week are absent this week, and others take their places. The Chicago *Times*, however, is well represented at most of the important meetings. There were about two thousand members of the Sons of Liberty in " good and regular standing" in Chicago alone, at the time they were let down. By careful arrangements we were able to have reports from the different temples throughout the most important points in the Northwest, and carefully noted the chief business and obtained the list of members, all of which has been as carefully placed in the hands of the authorities of the War Department, and months ago much of the information was imparted to Maj. Gen. Joseph Hooker, in command of the Northern Department, who was pleased to express his highest appreciation of the services rendered, and a desire to have the investigation thoroughly made, that indisputable facts might be obtained, that truth and justice might be promoted and the interest of the country thereby protected. So thorough and searching has been the investigation that *every* man of any note in this order, in almost every locality where this moral cancer has existed, is known and may consider himself in future upon his good behavior.

It was the policy of the Sons of Liberty, which they observed as far as it was possible for them to do, to obtain positions of trust in the army, upon the police, in the courts, in railway offices and telegraph stations, in the office of Provost Marshals, post-offices, departments of government, both local and general, indeed, so completely did they carry out this plan, that they made their boasts that they were represented upon all the railroads running out of Chicago, and it was not an unusual thing for them to report matters of the various departments just mentioned. One member of the Chicago Order, as appeared in evidence before the military commission, traveled over the North wherever he desired, on the pass of a Provost

Marshal in Indiana, his business being to aid in the organization of Temples in the different sections of the West. So rapidly did they increase in numbers, that Judge Morris estimated the number in Illinois alone at 80,000 members.

It was a rule of the organization, that its members should all be well armed and skilled in the use of weapons. The rapidity of increase in numbers, rendered them conscious of their strength, and they became openly defiant and talked treason upon the corners of our streets, and wherever little groups of people assembled. The mob spirit was excited, and all were ready for mischief whenever opportunity offered; and while all were bound to wait submissively till their leaders should give the signal for revolution, still many were restless and impatient for the hour to come, and hoped that they would not long have to wait. The suppression of the Chicago *Times* was an auspicious moment for them, and they made capital of it. They were never tired of talking of Vallandigham, and while that worthy staid in Canada he was very serviceable to the Order, as John Rogers was of more service to the church dead than while living. Vallandigham made an excellent martyr and an accomplished exile, but as an active member at home, old Doolittle, or Charles W. Patten, or James A. Wilkinson, or J. L. Rock, or Obadiah Jackson, Jr., Esq., or even Mrs. Morris herself, was worth two just like him. Why he could not have staid in Canada for the good of the cause, we cannot understand. What a Mecca was Windsor, and how great was Mahomet, but alas, when the great, the Hon. Clement Vallandigham relapsed into the three-cent fourth-class lawyer, in the little one horse city of Dayton, "what a fall was there my countrymen." No more pilgrimages, no more dinners with the great exile, no more texts of "arbitary arrests" to preach from, that could draw as Val used to draw.

The reception of the news of a victory by the rebels, was always an occasion of rejoicing among the Sons and Knights, and in the exuberance of their joy they shouted their treason in all sorts of places, and at all seasons. They assumed to be peace men, and yet were always ready for a quarrel. It became evident to all who kept posted in politics, that there would be a wide division between the different wings of the Democracy at the coming National Convention, and a most determined effort was to be made by the Peace faction, to control the action of the Convention, and long before the assembling of that body, newspaper strife had commenced between them, and it was hoped, and so it proved, that like the Kilkenny cats, they devoured each other. With Peace in their mouths and contention in their hearts, the "unterrified" resolved upon a great meeting, to be held in Peoria. It was a "big thing." The Chicago delegation took for the calumet of peace several boxes of fire-arms, so that if opportunity offered they might conquer a peace. Whiskey and gunpowder were other elements of that meeting, and as the escape of gas in petroleum wells, so noisy for a time, finally subsides, so after the ebulition at Peoria, Brig.-Gen. Walsh, and all the Chicago delegates, returned home, bringing with them their fire arms, without breaking bulk, and these weapons were carefully deposited, where they could instantly be obtained at the time of the uprising.

CHAP. VI.

MEETING OF THE SUPREME COUNCIL F. O. S. L. AT THE RICHMOND HOUSE, CHICAGO—TWO MILLION DOLLARS DISBURSED AS CONSIDERATION FOR THE GOOD OF THE ORDER—TRAITORS TO BE KNOWN TO EACH OTHER BY BADGES, AND THEIR PROPERTY SAVED BY DISPLAYING THE CONFEDERATE FLAG.

We have already shown that the three degrees in the Sons of Liberty had each their specific province. The lower strata composed of the rough material from which the Grand Council was made up by selections or choice of the brighter and more shining lights,—persons whose political views were up to the standard of treason, whose qualifications of intellect, shrewdness, cunning, caution, promptness, and firmness of purpose fully met the requirements of this degree of the order. The Supreme Council was composed of the Supreme Commanders—the ruling spirits of the order. This council was the body, therefore, from which all important measures must emanate, and the secrecy of their movements, even from the order below them, except such business as was regularly transmitted, was quite equal to that of the lower order, from the rest of the world. Such being the nature and character of this royal degree, and the fact that an uprising had been determined upon, it will be seen how essential it was to the Government of the United States, to be advised of their plans, and the the old adage that "where there is a will there is a way," was not a fallacy in the present case. On or about the 20th of July, 1863, agreeably to a private notice which had been extended to the Supreme Council, a meeting of that body was convened at the Richmond House, Chicago. During that day, as well as on the day preceding, members of that organization arrived in the city, and among the notables present on that occasion was Col. Barrett, who was a Major-General of the Sons of Liberty, in command of the District of Illinois, but who on the present occasion appeared in another character of no less moment, that of representative of the Confederate States Government, and charged with certain important instructions. Among the members present were Captain Majors, from Canada; Brig. Gen. Charles Walsh, of Chicago; Judge Bullitt, of the Supreme Court of Kentucky, who acted as Chairman; Dr. Bowles, Mr. Swan, Mr. Williams, Mr. Green, Mr. Piper, Mr. Holloway, H. H. Dodd and James B. Wilson, Auditor of Washington County, Indiana. The last named person and Mr. Green were present as members of Dr. Bowles' staff. After considerable discussion upon minor matters, Major-General Barrett, (commonly called Colonel Barrett, who had served the Rebel Government with some distinction, and was a first class rebel), made a formal proposition to unite Illinois, Kentucky, Missouri, Ohio and Indiana with the Confederate States, through the agency of the Sons of Liberty, and as to the other States, their relations would be an after consideration. The enterprise, he stated, would be attended with no little expense, and would necessarily involve extreme caution, prudence and firmness. He added, that the Southern Confederacy had placed in his hands the snug little sum of two millions of dollars, which had been captured from a Federal paymaster on the Red River, in Arkansas, to be applied in furtherance of this proposition. Captain Majors was also, by his own statement, a representative of the Rebel Government. It was proposed to distribute the two millions of dollars through the Grand Commanders of Indiana, Ohio, Kentucky, Missouri and Illinois, and that the money was by them to be distributed through the Major-Generals to the subordinate officers, according as might be deemed expedient. This money, says Mr. Wilson, (and we have the best of reasons to credit his statement,) was expended for arms.

Well do we remember that an oral report was submitted one evening at the Temple of the Illini, by the Grand Seignor presiding, that the pro rata for Illinois had been so expended, and that the weapons had been started for their destination, which was Chicago. These arms consisted of muskets, carbines, pistols, pistol belts and ammunition. At the Council meeting, of which we have spoken, the whole subject of revolution was freely discussed, and received the unanimous support of all present, and a time was named and agreed upon, but not until after much debate, several dates being named by different parties, and reasons given for fixing upon each. It was arranged that the Order in Indiana were to rendezvous at Indianapolis, also at Evansville, New Albany (opposite Louisville,) and Terra Haute, that they would seize the arsenal at Indianapolis, and the arms and ammunition would be distributed among the members. Wilson, before the military commission in Cincinnati, states that he learned from Dr. Bowles, that it was the purpose of the Order to free the rebel prisoners at Indianapolis, and that the same had been agreed upon with respect to other rebel camps, in other States, on the supposition that they would unite with the Sons of Liberty, in overturning the Government, and if they were found willing to do this, arms were to be placed in their hands. At that meeting it was a matter of discussion in what manner it was feasible to communicate with Gens. Buckner and Price, in order that they might co-operate, and have their forces near St. Louis and Louisville. The approach of their troops to those cities was the favored moment for beginning hostilities in the North. Mr. Wilson testified that he received a thousand dollars of the two million fund, but that instead of appropriating it according to the programme, he used it for buying substitutes, but the rightful owner can have the same upon call. Maj.-Gen. Barrett, the party having the fund in trust, has left the country, doubtless for his *health*, and the thousand dollars is still without

At this memorable meeting, as it was the last meeting of this body ever held in Chicago, it was agreed that at the time of the uprising, friends (rebels and copperheads) should appear with red and white badges, and the property of such persons would also be saved from destruction by displaying from their buildings the Confederate flag. Thus were ample and definite arrangements made, and as that meeting adjourned it was the deliberate end and aim of all the persons there assembled (with a single exception) to effect their objects at all hazards. All who were present, as well as the rebels then in Richmond, conceded that of all points in the several States embraced in the proposition with which Col. Barrett was entrusted, Chicago was by far the most important post, and the one which, of all others, should first fall. The facility and ease with which Camp Douglas could be taken, was a matter of remark among the traitors in every section, and it was understood that communication could readily be made with the prisoners, as Mrs. Morris, wife of Judge Morris, and others who were known to be in the interest of the Confederacy, had never been denied access to the camp, and such prohibition was scarcely expected, as of course the plans of the conspirators must be a dead secret from the commander of the post. In the temples of the Sons of Liberty it was a matter of congratulation that it was impossible for a detective to obtain their secrets, yet all this time Col. B. J. Sweet was well acquainted with every move that had the least importance, for the writer made it an invariable custom to send dispatches regularly to Col. Sweet, who thus came into full possession of the plans and designs of the Order, as soon as they were announced, and hence was at all times in a position that he could not have been surprised by any assault upon the Camp. The Colonel is at all times perfectly cool and self-possessed, prudent in the highest degree, and inflexible in purpose, when once resolved upon a line of action. His arrangements were made with all celerity and completeness, and though his little force was quite too small to offer great resistance in case of surprise had not the facts been known to the commandant, yet the interior arrangement of the camp, the disposition of his forces, and above all, the perfect discipline which had ever been maintained by him, now offered a silent barrier which caused the conspirators to entertain direful apprehensions, as to the disaster to themselves when they should make the undertaking, for the movements of the camp were noticed from the observatories near by, and on one occasion Brig. Gen. Walsh, accompanied by an attaché of the Chicago *Times*, made a personal visit to the camp, and being received as gentlemen by the gallant Colonel, they were able to make certain discoveries of a disagreeable nature. The greatest precaution, of course, was observed in the transmission of dispatches by the writer to Col. Sweet, for had it been supposed for a moment, that the commander of the post was cognizant of their acts, it would most certainly have precipitated the uprising, as the leaders of the conspiracy could not hope for so favorable a time again. The camp was enclosed by only one thickness of inch boards, not over twelve feet high, and a little force of less than eight hundred men were to guard some eight or ten thousand prisoners, many of them being the lowest class of raiders and ruffians.

During the latter part of July, at a meeting of the Sons of Liberty, Colonel Walker, of Indiana, was present, and in a speech referred to the recent seizure of arms in Iudiana, and said a formal demand had been made upon Governor Morton of that State for them, and if they were not forthcoming they (the copperheads) would compel restitution by the bullet, and said Morton would be assassinated if he refused. At this time a man named James A. Wilkinson was Grand Seignior of the temple. The question of supplying our quota to avoid the draft, agitating the community, it was proposed to resist the draft, and all the members were required forthwith to arm themselves with firearms, and Charles W. Patten and Wilkinson both offered to supply all who could not afford to purchase firearms. Wilkinson was a very efficient member of the order, and very zealous. Much of his time he passed in the organization of temples in different sections of country; and it was often stated as encouragement for the members that the temples were rapidly multiplying, and being filled with the "best kind" of men. It was earnestly requested of the members, as the time was short—Judge Morris saying the purposes of the organization would be fulfilled within the next sixty days—to bring in as many new members as possible, and the injunction was duly heeded. The temple in Chicago thrived remarkably, and arrangements were made by which individuals could initiate members, and the initiated increased in numbers rapidly.

CHAP. VII.

TIME FIXED FOR THE UPRISING OR REVOLUTION—EXTENSIVE PREPARATIONS—DRILL AND DISCIPLINE OF CLUBS—OPEN THREATS UPON OUR STREETS—MASS MEETINGS AND TARGET PRACTICE OF TRAITORS—PREPARATIONS FOR THE NATIONAL DEMOCRATIC CONVENTION IN CHICAGO—WHY THE UPRISING DID NOT TAKE PLACE—PRICE BEHIND TIME—ANOTHER PERIOD FIXED—ALL READY AT THE CONVENTION—PROMPT AND TIMELY PRECAUTION BY COLONEL SWEET.

The approach of the time fixed for the general uprising, witnessed remarkable and very unusual activity among the members of the Sons of Liberty, who now saw vividly the complete realization of their wishes, and were all, rank and file, in obedience to orders, busy with preparations. Little did the busy bustling city know of the plans and movements on foot. The same activity in trade, the same hopeful spirit among Union persons, the same gatherings at amusements, the same busy hum of industry as ever; nothing gave evidence of the existence of the terrible plot so soon to culminate, and to destroy by a single blow the hopes of our people,—to inaugurate a reign of terror as fearful as any in the history of the war. Citizens met and congratulated each other upon Union victories, and upon the probable speedy close of the national strife, and at the firesides of home discussed the terrible ravages of war, and as they knelt at the family altar, thanked God that our own city, and our State, and our section of the Union, had thus far been spared the immediate horrors and desolation which ever mark the theatre of warfare. Who of all in our fair city, besides the guilty wretches who were plotting the ruin and slaughter, had even a foreboding of the trouble so nearly upon them. For rebels in arms to commit cruelties and barbarities would have been expected, but for the authors of our ruin to be our very friends and neighbors, persons associated with us in business avocations, in social relations, and in the enjoyment of the same general blessings with ourselves, surpassed belief; yet such was the fact, and the faces that beamed smiles upon us by day, and joined us in our congratulations for national victories, by night were hideous with the dark designs and murderous intent. The gunsmiths were busy, and trade in weapons of all kinds was brisk; revolvers and knives particularly were articles of demand. So brisk and yet so silently and secretly, was the arming of individuals carried on, that weeks before the Convention assembled, but few, if any, of the members of Copperhead organizations but were well armed, and many had arms with which to supply other persons who might be less fortunate than themselves. It was indeed a dark picture to look in upon a group of the Sons of Liberty in their secure retreats, in the quiet hours of night, cleaning, repairing and inspecting their muskets and revolvers, moulding bullets, and making other preparations, and realizing that the mission of these monsters was the murder of men who dared proclaim and maintain their devotion to the Union. Upon the streets treason became emboldened, as time rolled on, and not a few personal collisions occurred from its utterance.

All this while that contemptible print, the Chicago *Times*, was instilling treason into the minds of its readers, and doing all that it could to embarrass the Government, discourage patriotism, and to give aid and comfort to the rebels; our victories, with that sheet, were always unimportant; our cause was unholy; our President a despot; our Union soldiers were hirelings; our Union-loving citizens were abolition fanatics; Jeff Davis was a master spirit of the age; his generals the heroes of the *Times;* and rebel victories were events cheering and hope giving, as they presaged the close of the war and peace; peace at the sacrifice of the Union, of national honor, of national dignity and national interests. Such was the Chicago *Times* at that period—the darkest era in our history—and as well might we have looked for mercy from a hyena, or reason from a ghoul, as in the event of open insurrection in our city, to have looked to Wilbur F. Story, editor of the *Times*, to have endeavored to suppress the flames his incendiary print had for years been fanning into a blaze. And yet, citizens of Chicago and the West, this same Chicago *Times*, *now*, after the occupation of Richmond by our forces, and the surrender of Lee and all his forces, and the end of the rebellion is at hand, this same Chicago *Times* pretends to rejoice in our success, and some days turns a cold shoulder upon its old friend and patron, who has contributed to its circulation and prosperity for years—Jeff Davis—and really declares that his master's cause is hopeless. Most noble Story, most patriotic Story, most consistent Story! Rather weep with the fallen fortunes of your masters. Flatter not yourself that the cloak of loyalty, which you have found it so convenient to fling around you, as our Union processions come marching along with thundering tread, that they will believe your conversion sincere and lasting; the cloak is not long enough to conceal your feet, and Union men will recognize the same Wilbur F. Story, and none will be so obtuse as not to discover under any disguise Bottom, the tailor. In the position of that Copperhead print, the state of mind of the *Times* man reminds us of an instance of what may be called poor consolation, A soldier of a division, after the command had run two days from the scene of an engagement, had thrown away his gun and accoutrements, and alone in the woods sat down and commenced thinking—the first opportunity he had for doing so. Rolling up his sleeves, and looking at his legs and general physique, he thus gave utterance to his feelings: "I am whipped—badly whipped—and somewhat demoralized, but no man, thank God, can say I'm scattered!" And so the Chicago *Times*, though kicked out of respectable society long ago, continues to print its daily issues, while from the scarcity of Copperheads all at once, since our recent glorious victories, we infer that *they* have been "scattered;" and as snakes cast their skins in the spring, so the Copperhead *Times* seems to have cast its own this season; but though it may appear in more pleasing garb with its present covering, let none forget that it is the same old Copperhead still. And the time will come when some enterprising showman will obtain and exhibit the last issue of that delectable sheet as the acme of treason and corruption during the war, and as an illustration of what villiany the mind of man may conceive, when he once turns against his country.

About the period of which we write, say a month prior to the Convention, informal meetings of the Sons of Liberty were frequent, and large numbers of the members often went out of the city on excursions, nominally for pleasure, but really for practice with fire arms. The most active preparations were made by the Democrats, resident of Chicago, to be able to accommodate their brethren from abroad, who would attend the Convention, or who would pay them an earlier visit; for the time of the uprising, it will be remembered, had been fixed for about the middle of August. The time assigned arrived, but "all was quiet on the Potomac," and along the placid and fragrant Chicago. It was a complete fizzle, but not from want of harmonius action on the part of the Copperheads of the Northwest, but to the chagrin of the Rebel government, Gen. Price failed to make his appearance in the vicinity of St. Louis, or Buckner about Louisville. The disappointment and vexation of the Sons of Liberty was great, and it found expression in the peculiar style of oratory and diction, which Judge Morris had introduced into the Temple. The failure of the rebels to concur, as had been arranged, was for a time quite inexplicable and unsatisfactory to the most ultra secesh of the Temple. It was not easy to communicate with Price and Buckner, and much mystery and doubt hung over the failure. The leaders were in doubt as to the wisdom of rising at the Convention, some being in favor and others adverse to it. It was evident the leaders were not a little embarrassed, but they finally agreed that a large force of "bone and muscle" should be on hand in Chicago at the Convention, and if it was found that the War Democrats should be in the ascendency, and the Peace wing could get nothing—either platform or candidate—the uprising should occur at that time, but so confident were the Peace men that they should be able to have the control of the Convention, that Judge Morris and Brig.-Gen. Walsh, and other leaders, announced to the members of the *Illini* their entire belief that there would be no doubt of the success of the Peace wing, in that Convention, and if so, no insurrectionary movement would be expedient; but if the uprising did not occur then, it surely would at the time of the Presidential election, and in the time which would elapse between the Convention and the election, the most active and earnest efforts would be made to strengthen the numbers of the Temples of the Sons of Liberty, wherever they existed. Judge Morris had expressed the confident belief that no difficulty would occur at the Convention, but declared if they (the Copperheads) should meet with any interferance, the most serious results would follow.

The rank and file who had been edified by such men as J. L. Rock, Charles W. Patton, James A. Wilkinson, L. C. Morrison, L. A. Doolittle, James Geary, Mr. Duncan, Mr. Dooley, Mr. Frank Adams, City Attorney, and many others were most impatient, and it was quite probable that a slight cause of offence with Union men would result in an open riot, that could not be suppressed till the grand aim of the Order was accomplished. About this time L. A. Doolittle, who was never tired of expressing his devotion to the distinguished exile Mr. Vallandigham, announced that Mr. V., who was Supreme Commander of the whole Order, would honor the Chicago Temple with a visit during the Convention, but that worthy could not find time to make the visit. As the excitement of the coming Convention seized upon the minds of those who were to participate in it, much speech making was done inside the Temples. At these meetings the writer particularly noticed two members, who seemed to have fallen into disfavor by the course which they had seen fit to adopt. One of these men was Christopher C. Strawn, a young lawyer of this city, of some education, a very fair order of talents, and who had seemed hitherto taciturn and reserved. Upon conversation with him we were astonished to find that he did not approve of the Jeff. Davis principles, and had no fellowship with any overt act of treason. He had been appointed a Brigadier-General, on the ground of his supposed ability, but early took occasion to express himself, in such a manner that his commission was speedily revoked. Mr. Strawn was, he declares, not in the clique who favored a revolution. Mr. Strawn was subsequently arrested, but he was soon released, and freely communicated truthful information to the authorities.

During the summer an event truly unfortunate for the Sons of Liberty took place, it being an exposé in the Chicago *Tribune* of the signs, grips, passwords, &c. of the order. This was a cause of great distress of mind. We remember that at a meeting about the 25th of August (Charles W. Patton presiding), the expediency of changing the signs, grips, &c. was considered, inasmuch as it would be unsafe to use them in public, but the lateness of the day, and the time drawing so near when the entire forces of the order would be called into requisition, it was not deemed expedient to undertake any change or modification. At this meeting Judge Morris made a speech in which he said that a demand had been made for arms seized in Indiana (as Col. Walker had proposed to do), and if the demand failed, the revolution would be begun in Indiana "as sure as there was a God in heaven or an abolitionist in hell."

At a meeting of the Chicago Temple Sons of Liberty, on the eve of the Convention, we heard for the first time (and that from the mouth of L. A. Doolittle), a definite plan for the attack of Camp Douglas. Doolittle told how the camp was situated, and that it was accessible on two sides; that guns were in position on only one side, and the west side was referred to by him as being the weakest; he spoke of the common board fence which formed the enclosure, and of the ease with which the camp could be taken, and the vast importance of liberating the prisoners the first thing upon an uprising. The speech of Doolittle was variously received;

many of the members were much interested; others who were in the higher degrees of the order were vexed beyond measure that Doolittle should be so stupid as to proclaim, in this public manner, a matter which really belonged to higher degrees of the organization to decide. One of the number, James Geary, a second-hand clothes dealer and broker on Wells street, who will receive further mention by and by, became so much incensed that he ordered Mr. Doolittle to his seat, declaring, with an oath, that Doolittle was telling too much.

At a meeting about this time, several of the members spoke upon the subject of releasing the prisoners at Camp Douglas. A map of Camp Douglas was exhibited by an individual present, who seemed to be a soldier. The map was a fine piece of work and had been made by a hand accustomed to such labor. Upon this map the precise position of the various departments, headquarters, cannon, &c., were laid down. There could be no shadow of doubt in the mind of any man not stupified with whiskey, and possessed of common sense, that the details of the attack had been carefully considered by those who were most interested in leading it on.

It had for some time been the policy of the Sons of Liberty to unite with the Invincible Democratic Club and the various McClellan escorts in the city and elsewhere, and seek to become its officers, that in case of an outbreak it would be far better to be the controlling power, than to be controlled. This plan worked admirably, and the Democratic Invincible Club of Chicago became one of the most corrupt organizations outside the order of Sons of Liberty. Its secretary at one time was Charles W. Patten, who had been a Grand Seignior of the Chicago Temple, was also a member of the Grand Council, and had taken a very active part in the prosperity of the order, and was chairman of the committee to see that all the Sons of Liberty were armed. One of the officers of the above named Club was Capt. P. D. Parks, whose devotion to Jeff. Davis and good whiskey were noticeable features in his character. This Capt. Parks was captain of the Invincible Club and often made speeches in the Sons of Liberty Hall.

On Saturday the 26th August (two days prior to the National Democratic Convention), immense numbers of persons came flocking to Chicago, indeed at no former time in the history of the city was there such an influx of strangers; they came in the cars and in wagon trains, and on horseback. One county alone sent nearly a thousand men. It was a noticeable fact that almost all persons who came into the city were well armed, and some of them even brought muskets. Treason was now rampant, and it would not be difficult, in looking around upon the most unprepossessing groups, and to hear the language, to fancy one's-self in Charleston, or some other nest of treason. From all the men who came to the city we did not, in a single instance, hear one good, hearty expression of Unionism, but our "Southern brethren and their rights," and this "wicked war," &c., &c., were the topics of conversation, and it was safe to set it down, that this was the Peace wing of that most remarkable bird,—Democracy of 1864.

The writer was in close communication with Col. Sweet, commandant at Camp

Douglas, and by aid of our auxiliaries not an item of information concerning the hostile intentions of the party transpired, that was not known instantly by Col. Sweet,—special carriers or orderlies conveying our dispatches. It must not be supposed that our observations were confined to Chicago. Our channels of communication with the principal points in the West were unobstructed; our "telegraphic cable" was in fine working order, and if those wise heads for a moment fancied that Col. B. J. Sweet might be caught napping, they were the worst self-deceived men we have ever seen. Col. Sweet proceeded with all caution and celerity to make his arrangements, and we beg the Colonel not to regard it as a breach of confidence in us to say, that the guns were in such a position and so well managed, that had there been any attempt to have assaulted the camp, there would not have been able-bodied traitors enough left, to have carried the killed and wounded to secure retreats. Almost any officer, perhaps, less cool than Col. Sweet would have blustered about in such a manner as to have rendered himself not only positively offensive to the citizens, but would have placed the city under martial law, and doubtless precipitated the very event it was wise for a time to avert. Col. Sweet was cool, and managed the matter with the most perfect military ability and skill. He compelled everybody, friend and foe, to respect him by his dignified, gentlemanly bearing, and yet there was that about his appearance that told plainer than words, that while he was courteous, polite, kind and willing to do all in his power and consistent with his duty to preserve the peace, yet had an outbreak been begun, of all men in Chicago, rebels and sympathisers would prefer to get as far as possible from Col. Sweet, or the reach of his influence. This gallant officer had his men under such perfect discipline that a simple request, even when the men were not on duty, was obeyed with the alacrity as if it had been a peremptory order. The discovery that Col. Sweet was ready for them, which discovery was early made and duly reported, had much to do with the good order which prevailed in Chicago during the Convention.

CHAP. VIII.

TIME OF THE DEMOCRATIC NATIONAL CONVENTION—TREASON EVERY-
WHERE PREVALENT—INSIDE VIEW OF THE TEMPLE OF SONS OF
LIBERTY—MAJ.-GEN. BARRETT WITH COMMISSION FROM JEFF. DAVIS,
AT THE HEAD OF A TORCHLIGHT PROCESSION IN CHICAGO—TRAITORS
WITH LOADED MUSKETS UPON OUR STREETS.

The extraordinary activity of recruiting for the Sons of Liberty, and the zeal displayed by the master spirit of the Temple was ominous of the wicked work they might be called upon to perform. James A. Wilkinson, who was elected Grand Senior, was too young a man in the estimation of many, and he was about to resign, when Judge Morris remarked, that "age was not always wisdom" (the truth of which his own career has fully illustrated,) and by request Wilkinson continued to hold the post. The old order for arming of members was called up, and all were required to comply with the condition at once; a particular pattern of revolvers was specially recommended, and it was ascertained that the members were in almost every instance, fully armed. A young man named R. T. Semmes, who was said to be a near relative to the commander of the rebel pirate Alabama, was appointed to deliver an address before the Order, but this duty was never complied with in a formal manner, as it was subsequently thought Judge Morris was better qualified, he being in a higher degree than Mr. Semmes, to impart such information as the lower degree should know. Upon an occasion of a special meeting, the Judge made a long address, in which he stated the number of members of the Order in Illinois at 80,000 men, saying they were all well drilled and could be implicitly relied upon, at the right time; members were enjoined to remember their obligations to sustain the principles of the Order, and to aid each other. The Judge stated that "we" (the Sons of Liberty,) had *two full regiments* all well armed and drilled, in Chicago, and that a third was forming. Such cheering information was received with great gratification, and gave a greater impetus to the recruiting for the Order.

The question of the draft agitated the members at each meeting, and all declared their purpose never to go to the army, either voluntarily or otherwise, to fight our brethren, "whose cause was just and right," and a strong attempt was made to array the organization by formal action to oppose the Government, and those especially who were impatient for the general uprising, thought it a timely opportunity and ample provocation, and felt confident that as the South manifested open hostility and presented a bold and united front instantly upon the firing of the first gun upon Fort Sumter, so would it be in all the States of the Northwestern league; they would at once rise, when knowing that their brethren of Chicago were in arms against the "usurper and his hirelings;" but these hasty counsels did not prevail, and individuals were exhorted to take care of themselves if drafted, but on no account to go to the army.

Not only was there remarkable activity in the Chicago Temple just prior to the Convention, but in all the States where the order existed. Our Indiana neighbors often sent their worst Copperheads to the Chicago Temple to receive instructions in regard to the mode of initiation; and about this time, a man named Westfall, of Elkhart, Indiana, appeared in the Temple, and edified the members with most encouraging accounts of the order in his own State. He was properly qualified as a Grand Seignor, and no doubt served with that grace and dignity of which his appearance gave such promise. It is hoped that the citizens of Elkhart appreciate this gentleman's devotion to "the great cause." Judge T. H. Marsh was put through a similar course of training, and being possessed of remarkable dignity, no doubt made an excellent Grand Seignor. If he was not fit for a good Judge, he was fit for a Son of Liberty. He no doubt remembers the artist, who by an unlucky daub, spoiled his picture of an angel, but took fresh courage, declaring it would make an excellent devil. So the judge may make his own application.

The day of the great Convention at length dawned upon at least a hundred thousand strangers in Chicago. Every hotel was densely packed from cellar to garret, private houses were filled to their uttermost capacity, while hundreds the night before, who could not find any kind of a shelter, took in plenty of whisky to prevent catching cold, and laid themselves quietly at rest in the gutters, much to the consternation of the myriads of rats that infest our streets. These street sleepers now arose, and shaking themselves, their toilet was complete. Of all the God-forsaken, shaggy-haired, red-faced, un-shorn, hard-fisted, blasphemous wretches that have ever congregated, even at the gallows at Newgate, many of the visitors of the Peace wing of the Democracy were entitled to the first consideration. Still there was no collision with the citizens, although the representatives of the "unterrified" had sworn that there should be no arrests in Chicago during the Convention. The better class of strangers were War Democrats, and it was evident they had no fellowship for the ragmuffins of the Peace wing.

It should here be stated that the Order of the Sons of Liberty had purchased firearms, carbines, pistols, shot guns and rifles, and at the time of the Convention had stored in the city of Chicago, arms, for at least ten thousand men. These arms had been brought here at various times; some of them had been brought by vessels and others by rail, and were now safely deposited in four different depots in Chicago, the locations of which were known only to the Sons themselves. From these four principal depots one or more boxes of arms were taken on such occasions as would best serve, and placed in trust with some out-and-out rebel sympathizer in the different wards, so that at the time of the general uprising the "faithful" could readily obtain supplies. On one occasion Brig.-Gen. Walsh applied to H. A. Phelps, on State street, with a request for him to receive two boxes of muskets, but that man did not like to incur the risk, whatever his sympathies may have been, and the arms were not deposited with him.

It was quite apparent, the first day of the Convention, that our citizens had resolved to act upon the advice of Adjutant-General Fuller, to let these fellows "have their jaw out," and they did have it out, and became terrible *bores*.

At an early hour, the temporary building erected for this gathering, near Michigan Avenue, was crowded to excess, and after beginning their labors all the speakers, without exception, entertained the audience and relieved themselves of the most violent denunciations of President Lincoln, and the policy of the administration. Each speaker vied with the last in culling from his vocabulary of hard words, terms sufficiently expressive of their feelings toward the government, but do as well as they might, even with the aid of the poorest quality of whiskey and education, evidently of many years among the lowest of the low, not one of them could out-do the Chicago *Times*. The only parties who could approximate it were Gov. Harris of Maryland, and Long of Ohio, who were most decidedly in favor of secession. The differences between the War Democrats and the Peace men, well nigh ended in personal violence, and would, but for timely interference of the police. It is not our purpose to report the doings of the Convention, and an allusion is only made to call special attention to the elements which made up the party who gave to General George B. McClellan a nomination which proved to him the worst punishment that could have been inflicted, and exhibited him to the world in worse company than he had ever before mingled. The hostility between the different factions of the party, but rendered the Peace wing or Sons of Liberty the more united, and more firmly bent upon the overthrow of the government, as they saw clearly enough, even before the adjournment, that there was not a shadow of hope of electing the ticket formed, and the only hope of genuine copperheads now laid in the election of State officers, and Judge Morris told the people "if we can but get our Governor and Lieut.-Governor, it is all we ask for; the order is strong enough in Illinois, Indiana, Kentucky, Missouri, Iowa and Ohio to enable us to take the general government into our own hands." He added, "as the Washington government had not seen fit to execute the Constitution and the laws, we will bring them to Illinois and execute them ourselves."

At the close of the Convention, and the compromise had been made by the different factions of the party, then came a time for general rejoicing. In the evening torchlight processions, with lanterns and transparencies bearing devices and mottos, all expressive of their animosity at the administration. At the head of one of these processions was Maj.-Gen. Barrett, the military commander of Illinois. At that very time Barrett had in his pocket a programme, which had an intimation been received from Price or Buckner, would have been of fearful import to the citizens of Chicago. Barrett had at one time lived in Chicago, but for some months past was a resident of Missouri. He was thoroughly armed, and well knew the elements that had assembled in the city. Barrett had been in the rebel service, or rather we should say in *another* arm of the service, inasmuch as none in these days, when all men are for the Union, and it is so easy to be a patriot, will pretend to deny that the Sons of Liberty were as much an arm of service for Jeff. Davis as his artillery or infantry. This fellow Barrett, had on one occasion, as appears by testimony before the Cincinnati military commission, visited Chicago as an accredited agent of the Davis government, but he was not molested, and mingled with men of his own stripe, without fear and without difficulty. It will be interesting by and by, to read of the Chicago Convention, and the incongruous elements there assembled. But as all things have an end, so did this remarkable gathering, and dispersed quietly, never again to meet as the representatives of the American people.

Of course most of the Roughs of the Peace wing had been induced to come to Chicago, with the idea that an uprising was imminent, and would no doubt take place, when they would be able to repay themselves abundantly from the property of our citizens. It is not strange therefore, that these half starved, brutal wretches looked with evil eyes upon our National banks, and hoped till the last that some lucky incident might occur which would provoke an outbreak, and they would have an opportunity to pillage our banks, stores and dwellings, but they were doomed to disappointment, and with surly looks and threats of vengeance, left the city, resolved at a future day to draw their pay, principle and interest, from our banks, and we shall, in a future chapter, see the manifestation of the same spirit, easily recognized as Peace wing democracy

CHAP. IX.

REBEL OFFICERS IN THE TEMPLES OF SONS OF LIBERTY—MURDERERS, BOUNTY JUMPERS, DESERTERS, FELONS, VAGABONDS AND TRAITORS IN COUNCIL—PLANS OF ATTACK ON CAMP DOUGLAS—FIRES TO BE KINDLED IN THE CITY—BANKS AND STORES TO BE ROBBED—NAMES OF SPEAKERS—HATRED OF UNION SOLDIERS.

At a meeting of the Sons of Liberty in September, 1864, a plan was reported, much to the relief of those who had a horror of conscription; it was arranged that such of the members as might be drafted, should report within three days to the Grand Senior of the Temple, and they would be supplied with means to defray their expenses to the southern part of the State, where they would remain till their services should be required, and that they would find friends there, strong enough in numbers, to defy the officers of the law. Such persons were to form military organizations, and to be drilled and disciplined by rebel officers sent thither for that express purpose. The "Sons" of Chicago expressed their extreme regret at the very open and defiant manner of their brethren in the southern part of the State, and believed that it would be predjudicial to the prosperity of the Order.

Our readers have not forgotten the Coles county tragedy, the murderers and their victims. There is not a particle of doubt that those murders were premeditated, and first the subject of discussion in the temples of the Sons of Liberty. The assault was made without provocation, and the thirst for the blood of Union men was the motive for the deed. We have never advocated or countenanced mob law, but if there was ever a time in the history of our government in which it was justifiable, it was in the cases of the Coles county murderers. The times seemed, perhaps, to have demanded a vigilance committee of citizens, who would administer justice fast enough to suit the emergency of the cases upon which they might be called to adjudicate, and having "cleaned out" the murderous scoundrels in that locality, they might have found a demand for their services in Chicago. But it is better that the people controlled their just indignation and left it to time, to punish the infamous wretches who turned their arms and their all against the country, to whom they are indebted for all the blessings which they proved themselves to be utterly incapable of appreciating. It was the boast of the "Sons" that their numbers embraced many of the officers of our armies, and the names of several were mentioned, who had sworn that they would never fire or order their commands to fire upon "our Southern brethren," and it was added that such officers could serve the cause of this order better in the field, than in any other manner.

As time passed on, the plans of the villains belonging to the Chicago Temple, or the plans of the order throughout the State for the attack upon Camp Douglas became more complete in their details. The policy of obtaining positions for members upon all the railroads and in telegraph offices, was very popular with the order, and it was confidently stated, that upon the release of the prisoners the leaders would at once take full possession of the railroads and telegraph offices. It was arranged that the attack upon the camp should be made the night after election, as it now became fully apparent to all that there was not a shadow of a chance to elect either National or State ticket by the Copperheads. Fires were to be kindled in different parts of the city, and these were to be so numerous that they would necessarily divert the attention of the citizens, while the attack should be made. Near the camp is a growth of small oaks and other small wood which offered a fine retreat or hiding place for those who would attack the camp. The attacking party were to go singly or in groups which might not attract attention, and when they were in readiness, they were suddenly to spring forward and commence an assault simultaneously on three sides of the enclosure. The risk to the invading party was not considered large, as the whole undertaking would be but the work of a few moments, and it was confidently believed that some communication could previously be established with the rebels by their desperate friends and allies upon the outside; and it is now quite certain that some intelligence was communicated to the rebels, and well understood by them, as not long before the election, supposed signals in the way of rockets, blue lights, &c. were at one time exhibited by a small group of persons, without any apparent design, which could have been distinctly seen at camp. Mrs. Morris, who has confessed her complicity with the rebel sympathizers, was a frequent visitor to the camp, and it was thought that she might be very useful in conveying letters, messages, &c. Indeed it was morally certain that there was an understanding between the rebels inside, and the cowardly dogs on the outside of the post. It will be remembered that fire arms for at least ten thousand men were safely and secretly stored in Chicago, and that there was a perfect understanding between the members of the higher degrees of the Sons of Liberty, and the leaders of the invading party from Canada. Had the attack been made, however good the understanding between the "Sons" and the rebels might have been, the former would soon have found, to their surprise and to their dismay, that their glory would suddenly have departed, for the released rebels would instantly have obeyed the commands of their own officers, and Northern Sons of Liberty would have been compelled to fall into line, whether they would or not. A few of the Sons would have received some consideration, and this would especially have been the case with Brig.-Gen. Charles Walsh, but in the main the "accursed democracy,"—as one rebel writing to another was pleased to speak of the order—was to be kept in the front, or in other words, used as circumstances might require to do the vilest offices of this vile and devilish conspiracy. As the time of the election was drawing near, the Sons of Liberty expressed a wish to have a man at their head, in the place of Wilkinson, who would command respect, and whose appearance of dignity and years would impress new comers most favorably. This man was found in Obadiah Jackson, Jr. Esq., as Grand Seignior, and so much gratified were they with his peculiar fitness for this distinguished honor, that they resolved to find a second officer, or Ancient Brother, and Lewis C. Morrison gave place to a Mr. Hoffman.

Things were now working smoothly, new members were rapidly joining, and it was evident that the new organization was most favorable for the growth and unity of the Order. The rapidly increasing number of Temples in every part of the State, would have been truly alarming to the friends of the Union. New comers were introduced at every meeting, and large numbers were initiated at Judge Morris' residence, where favored individuals were also initiated in the mysteries of the higher degrees; so that there were hundreds of persons, in good standing with the Order as bona fide members, who seldom or never visited the lodge room; this was especially the case with the higher grade of persons—the politicians, lawyers and others. At a meeting in the autumn, Judge Morris was present and made a speech in response to the request of several members, who asked information concerning the immediate purposes of the Order. He spoke, as was his custom, of the tyranny of the Pressdent; he said the rights of the people had been trampled upon, and the constitution had been violated by him. He referred to the suspension of the *habeas corpus*, and said many of our best men were at that moment "rotting in Lincoln's bastiles;" that it was our duty to wage a war against them, and open their doors; that when the Democrats got into power they would impeach and probably hang him, and all who were thus incarcerated should be set at liberty; that thousands of our best men were prisoners in Camp Douglas, and if once at liberty would "send abolitionists to hell in a hand basket;" he said the meanest of those prisoners was purity itself compared to "Lincoln's hirelings." He added that the tyranny of "Abraham the First" was fast drawing to a close, and those who were anxious to fight, would not have to wait long. He also spoke in favor of retaliation.

The Judge's speeches were always marked by vehemence, profanity and violent gesticulation; he never spoke except to condemn the administration, and to express his confidence in this Order to remedy all the evils of the administration, and that we should very soon—"in sixty days," have the power, and yet on several occasions he expressed the belief that McClellan would not be elected. No one, not even the most stupid in the first degree of the Temple, could fail to understand how the Copperheads were to have the reins of the General Government in sixty days, and yet that the party could not hope for success at the polls.

A man named William Hull, connected with the Order, rebuked such speeches in unqualified terms, and as a consequence drew down upon himself the odium of the Order. Mr. Hull expressed himself in favor of compliance with the Constitution and the laws, and of the Union. His denunciations of the rebels excluded him from the confidence of the leaders, who began to regard him as a "dangerous man," and expressed the belief that he would turn against them, and therefore required watching. Mr. Hull was a man of good common sense, and made several Union speeches in the Order, which confirmed the suspicion that had been expressed by some, that he was a spy and detective, and it was said it would be far better to *put him out of the way*, or in other words to kill him, lest he might betray them, and further as the time of the election was so near at hand, it was voted by the Sons of Liberty to destroy all their records, so that in case of arrest no documentary evidence could be brought against them. While the motion was pending, Mr. Richard T. Semmes, one of the prisoners tried at Cincinnati, moved an amendment, that the names of members be retained, so that in case any one should betray the Order they might be known and hung, but it was not deemed safe to preserve the record, and most of the memoranda was destroyed, but for the edification of the members, we will add that we have on deposite in Chicago an entire and correct list of names of the Chicago, and most of the prominent Temples, and it may be deemed expedient to publish it hereafter; this will be determined by the general behavior of the members themselves.

In regard to Mr. Hull, to whom we have alluded, it should be said that his death was fixed upon by the members. Felton and Morrison agreed to do the work, but afterwards another proposition was made, to give him money and induce him to leave for parts unknown. This peaceable disposition of the man was *not* satisfactory. Said they, "dead men tell no tales," and at an informal meeting, a vote was taken and all, with a single exception, present were in favor of *death*. That exception required more satisfactory evidence that Hull was the informer, and thus the murder of the man was prevented. The writer has not a particle of doubt, having been present at this meeting and heard the proposition and the vote taken, that the murder would have been perpetrated within twenty-four hours had not a single person been so exacting in regard to the facts. It may readily be believed that the writer never mingled in this murderous company without a brace of revolvers in his pocket, ready for instant use, and it may be no stretch of credulity to believe, that in case of an assault, the instruments would have been called into requisition.

About the first of October, the restrictions upon the purchase and sale of fire-arms were removed, and the trade in the city in this department became very active.

The intensity of hatred of Union soldiers, by the Copperheads would almost challenge credence. It was a common thing to seek to embroil them in personal altercations, and to fall upon them with violence and malice, and it is our opinion, that in almost every case where soldiers ever became involved in personal difficulty, the provocation came from Copperheads. We may mention an instance in point. During the summer, a Union soldier presented himself at our office and required surgical aid. His head was bleeding copiously, and his hair matted with blood,

COL. G. ST. LEGER GRENFELL,

"Who has fought in every clime, the man who advised raising the Black Flag and murdering Union soldiers, and who was to have assumed command of the Rebel prisoners upon being released from Camp Douglas, and to whom the citizens of Chicago would have had to appeal for mercy."

and so mutilated was he that he could scarcely speak or walk. He was perfectly sober, and evidently a very quiet, worthy man. It was doubtful how his injuries might terminate, but the poor fellow received our best attention, and thanks to a kind Providence, recovered after a long and painful illness. It appears that he was beset by a party of Copperheads, without the least provocation, only that he was a *Union soldier*. For our act of humanity in rendering professional aid, we were gravely suspected for a time of being "a dangerous man," and received several lectures of censure from the Sons of Liberty. He was but a "Union soldier," and his death, they said, was a matter of congratulation rather than of regret.

CHAP. X.

THE REASONS WHY REBEL AGENTS WERE SENT TO CANADA, AND THEIR DOINGS—VARIOUS PLOTS OF MISCHIEF, HARRASSING, PILLAGING, &c.—THE WATCHWORD OF THE REBELS IN CANADA.

The United States armies being continually pressed forward, step by step, towards the heart of the Confederacy, occupying more and more of the soil from which their commissary was but illy and scantily supplied, together with a desire on the part of the Southern people, to let the people of the North see what invasion meant, to make them feel and see the destruction and desolation following our army of invasion, determined the Richmond government, in 1863, to send its agents to the Canadas, well supplied with money, to endeavor to foment discord, and to intensify the dissatisfaction already existing in certain political circles, with the government, to such an extent that it could be made available for their own uses and purposes. Knowing that thousands of their soldiers were confined at Johnston's Island, and Camp Douglas near Chicago, almost within twelve hours' travel of Canada, it was the great object of the rebel government to release those prisoners of war, and in the mean time having stirred up and excited a formidable conspiracy in the North, particularly in the North-West, having in view the subversion of the government, and the securing of material aid and assistance to the rebels, and those rebel prisoners being released through the instrumentality of the rebels from Canada and those of the Northern sympathizers who could be induced to join in the expeditions for that purpose, the conspiracy was to culminate all over the North—but principally in Illinois, Ohio, Indiana, Kentucky, Missouri and New York, and effect the release of the prisoners of war confined in the various prisons in those States. The prisoners at all these places being released, were to form a nucleus around which all the dissatisfied people of the Northern States could rally, and endeavor to maintain themselves and their cause here in the North, and by rallying in formidable numbers, to cause the withdrawal of so many troops from the field in front, to establish peace at home, that it would materially change the whole character of the war, and remove the seat of war from the cotton States to the Northern States—Kentucky, Tennessee and Missouri. Upon the withdrawal of the troops in any considerable numbers from the front, was to follow the advance of the rebel armies into Kentucky, Tennessee and Missouri.

Sterling Price would never have invaded the State of Missouri in the fall of 1864, had it not been to give all the aid and assistance the rebellion could afford, to the conspiracy just then ready to break loose, and this explains the position that Hood occupied for nearly two months in Northern Georgia, Alabama and Tennessee. He would never have placed himself in such a position, had it not been deemed absolutely necessary by the Richmond Government, that his army should be placed where upon the breaking out of the conspiracy he could exercise a great influence over its prospects of success. To further the objects and views just stated, Jacob Thompson, of Miss., formerly Secretary of the Interior under Buchanan's administration, was made a secret agent for the Rebel Government in the Canadas, and two hundred and fifty or three hundred thousand dollars in specie, or its equivalent, was placed in his hands by the Rebel Government, for the purpose of arming and equiping any expedition he might place on foot from British America, for the injury of the inland or ocean commerce of the United States, or harrassing its Northern borders, and particularly for the release of the Rebel prisoners of war at Camp Douglas and Johnston Island, and from the beginning of Mr. Thompson's services in Canada, we may date all the regularly organized and officered expeditions from British America against the United States. Chief of all these expeditions were the two attempts, during last year, to release the prisoners of war at Camp Douglas, near Chicago, Ill., and the two different attempts to capture the steamer "Michigan" (a United States vessel of war stationed on Lake Erie, carrying eighteen guns), and release the prisoners on Johnston's Island. All four of these expeditions failed totally in the objects for which they were organized, mainly by some friendly parties having put the military authorities on their guard soon enough to enable them to defeat the attempts, and in some instances to capture the parties concerned in them.

To aid Mr. Thompson in his nefarious efforts in Canada, several officers of various ranks were detailed from the Rebel army, by the Richmond government, most prominent among these were Col. St. Leger Grenfell, an Englishman of great military experience and daring, and Capt. T. H. Hines, a young officer, who having been one of Gen. John A. Morgan's pets, was recommended by him for the position he held in Canada, but who was possessed of no more than ordinary military talents or genius, unless his shrewdness in getting other and better persons involved in difficulty, and condemned either to prison or death, and getting himself out, evidenced military prowess. In connection with these men, were a great many citizens, of both the United States and the South, who while they were not authorized to act in any way by the Rebel government, yet showed their zeal in the cause of the rebellion, by aiding and advising with Mr. Thompson, and advising and exhorting all the rebel soldiers in Canada, and the refugees from the Northern States, to take an active part in the different schemes there on foot, to harrass the northern border of the United States.

The most prominent of this class were George N. Sanders, C. C. Clay, formerly Representative in the United States Congress from Alabama, Col. Steele and Daniel Hibber. There was still another secret agent of the rebels on special duty in Canada, viz., Judge Holcombe of Virginia, who was sent there for the purpose of secretly establishing agencies for the returning of rebel soldiers, who desired to go South. However much Mr. Holcombe's mission removed him from military matters, he nevertheless approved of the different expeditions which were then being organized, and did more perhaps, than any one else, to cause the irritation now existing between the Canadians and the citizens of the United States.

His policy in establishing agencies in Canada, was to get some prominent and influential citizens of the country who sympathized with his government, to act as agents to furnish rebel soldiers who had escaped to Canada, and who desired to return South, with all the necessary clothing, rations and money, &c., to enable them to go to Montreal or Quebec, where there were regularly established rebel agencies, who upon the arrival of such soldiers so furnished with money, for all the money so advanced, with perhaps interest, was returned. In this way Mr. Holcombe enlisted, besides the feelings, the interests of a great many prominent business men, whose means had been advanced to rebels, and all along the Grand Trunk and Great Western railway, in all the principal towns and cities, he succeeded in establishing such agencies, which although at first intended only for those who were rebel soldiers, finally became nothing more than recruiting rendezvous for the rebel army, which all the skedadlers, refugees from the Northern and Border States who wished to join the Southern army, were received, fed, clothed and quietly transported to the South.

Upon the departure of Mr. Holcombe south, his business was turned over to C. C. Clay, who after that acted in this capacity. It was during Holcombe's stay in Canada, that the speculative brain of George N. Sanders, first originated the great humbug of the Niagara Falls peace conference, at which there was but one rebel official, and he was not authorized to act in any such capacity. But the speculative Sanders, having lived like Barnum nearly his whole life, upon humbugs, made his last and greatest effort to humbug the American people, into the belief that the Southern people really desired peace, and that he Clay and Holcombe, although not regularly authorized by the Rebel government, still could speak for and influence the Southern people. While in reality the whole conference was nothing on the part of Sanders & Co., but the last act of a desperate political gamester, who ventured his all upon one last throw of dice, to win or lose it all. If Sanders, Holcombe, Clay and others, could have made the people of the North believe the South really desired peace, and that the only obstacle in the way was the obstinacy of the General Government, which did not desire it, but wished to annihilate the Southern people, they could have materially affected the then coming Presidential election in the North, and perhaps elected a Democratic president, who would have added to the disasters then affecting the country—general and complete ruin. The election of such a man as Gen. McClellan, at such a time, and professing such principles as actuated the Democratic party at that time, would have insured to the South her independence, rather than further war and a dismemberment of the Union. All this these parties professing to represent

Southern opinion well knew, and had they been successful, would have reaped a rich political reward.

Having endeavored to give a correct outline of the characters of the rebel leaders in Canada, and the different spheres in which they acted, it is now necessary to give some idea of the different classes of individuals who were led by such men, and prompted by them to undertake the many hair-brained expeditions, which they first plotted and started. These persons are rightfully and very expressively divided into four different and distinct classes : 1st. The Rebels. 2d. The skedaddlers. 3d. Refugees. 4th. Bounty jumpers and escaped criminals. The term rebel is applied only to persons who have been or are connected with the rebel army, and they again are subdivided into two classes; first, those rebels who have gone to Canada as a means of escape to the South; and, secondly, those who, having been accustomed to easy and luxurious living in times of peace, and having become thoroughly disgusted with service in the army, where they were subjected to strict military discipline, sought in Canada an asylum from compulsory service of both parties. 2d. Skedaddlers, as they are called, are those persons who having been drafted, or seeing a possibility of it, in the United States army, had fled to Canada to avoid the service. This class consisted mostly of fast young men, having either their own or the pockets of their parents well lined, and accustomed to live without labor of any kind, were not disposed to take a part on either side which would subject them to the inconveniences, hardships or privations of a soldier's life; and partly of persons who, while they sympathized with the rebellion, still did not care to make their precious bodies targets for the sake of upholding the principles which they professed to entertain. 3d. Refugees, or persons who, for the sake of expressing their opinions and feelings against the government, without fear of imprisonment, had removed to Canada where they could vent their spleen and malice against all things connected with the United States, and vaunt their pernicious principles under the protection of the outstretched paw of the British lion. 4th. Bounty jumpers and criminals who could not be pursued and brought back to this country for punishment under the existing extradition treaty between the United States and Canada. This last class exceeds by far all the others in point of numbers, and the low degree of infamy to which they are reduced—rebels skedaddlers, refugees and bounty jumpers, with a mixture of escaped criminals, forming an almost indescribable mass of people, from all nations, all climes, and of almost every imaginable description, and chiefly distinguished for being more frequently found in the bar-rooms, billiard saloons, gambling hells, &c.

CHAP. XI.

HE First Attempt to Release the Prisoners of War at Camp Douglas—The Character in which they came—Under the Lead of Capt. Hines—The Reasons why they failed to effect their object—Rebel Officers and Soldiers drilling Copperheads in Southern Illinois and Indiana.

It is the writer's intention to speak first of two expeditions to Chicago, for the release of the prisoners confined there. The first of these took place during the Chicago Democratic Convention, when it was hoped that the rebels from Canada and their sympathizers from Missouri, Kentucky, Indiana and Illinois, who came armed to assist them in their projects, would be enabled to go quietly into the city without fear of detection, in the vast crowds who were then assembling there, from all parts of the United States, and under the guise of friendly visitors, were to be ready at a moment's notice whenever their leaders called upon them to spring out before the people in their true light, and effect the release of those rebels confined at Camp Douglas. As early as the twenty-fourth and twenty-fifth of August last, at the request of Jacob Thompson, secretly and quietly circulated all through the Canadas, Nova Scotia and New Brunswick, all the Rebels, Skedaddlers, Refugees, and others who could be relied upon to take part in the expedition, began to assemble in Toronto, Canada West, at the different hotels and boarding houses; of these, at that time, it was generally reported that there were about three hundred; but so far as positive evidence goes, out of this number only about seventy-five men were induced to join this expedition and go to Chicago. At Toronto the objects of the expedition were made known to nearly all of them, and arms furnished them—*arms manufactured in New York city and shipped to Canada for that express purpose*. The details of the affair were only known to a few of the leaders, who maintained the strictest silence upon the subject, and enjoined upon the men the most implicit obedience to their orders, pledging themselves for their safety and the feasibility of their plans. On the nights of the twenty-sixth, twenty-seventh and twenty-eighth of August, these men began to leave Toronto, by all the different routes leading to Chicago, in squads of from two to ten, and began to arrive at the Richmond House in that city, as early as the Saturday before the Convention. They were all pledged to fight to the last, and never under any circumstances surrender, as their lives would be forfeited, if caught. The whole expedition was under the charge of Capt. Thomas H. Hines, who had a commission as Major-General in the Rebel army, to take effect and date from the release of the rebel prisoners of war at Rock Island or Camp Douglas. Hines is the person who is said to have effected the escape of General John H. Morgan himself, and others from the penitentiary at Columbus, Ohio, and although it is not generally known in the North or South how Morgan escaped, and there not being one word of truth in his report, he has enjoyed for a long time the reputation of having been the author of it, and of being a desperate shrewd character. The real facts in the case were (and it does not do the service of the United States much credit to mention them,) that General John H. Morgan "*was bribed out.*" It was absolutely necessary however for General Morgan to make some report of his escape to the public, that would hoodwink the United States Government and save the officers, whom his friends in the North had bribed to let him out, from punishment by the authorities, and therefore a very romantic tale was made up, and Morgan's pet *Capt. Hines*, was made the hero of it; and it was the object of the rebel government in sending Hines to Canada to give an air of truth to this romantic tale, to secure the United States officials who have failed in their duty to their country. Hines was assisted in his efforts by Col. St. Leger Grenfel an English adventurer of great military experience, personal bravery and daring, who has had a romantic connection with nearly every important war in America, Europe, Asia and Africa for the past thirty years, and served in the Southern army with the rank of Col., as Adjt.-Gen. to Morgan, and afterwards on General Bragg's staff; but who pretended to have resigned his commission in the rebel army and was living quietly in Canada; also by one Capt. Castleman of Morgan's command, from Kentucky, who acted as Quartermaster of the party, and about seventy-five, rank and file, (nearly all of whom were officers) of the rebel army from Canada. These men were to be met here in Chicago by parties from nearly all the middle, western and border States, who came armed like themselves and for the same purpose. Of those citizens who came to Chicago, armed and ready like the rebels, there were over a thousand persons organized and officered, camped in this city, just waiting for the command, and there were in the vast throng then assembled in Chicago five or six thousand, who, while they would not attach themselves to any organization, and were afraid to risk the first attempt, yet if the first attempt had been successful they would have joined the others in their work of devastation and destruction.

The above is most too low an estimate of the number of these malcontents who did not join any military organization, but would have eventually joined if it had been successful; for rebel officers have been heard to say in Canada, after the Convention was over, that if they could have "*started the thing right,*" they would have had an army of twenty-five thousand in a week. With such a force, or even a force of ten thousand, in possession of the city of Chicago, almost every city and large town where there were many Democrats, and where the Sons of Liberty, the Illinois Societies, Illini, &c., had full sway in Missouri, Kentucky, Indiana, Ohio and Illinois, were to raise the insurrectionary cry, and endeavor to bring all peace men and Democrats under their banners. They were also to endeavor to

JAMES A. WILKINSON,

Past Grand Seignior of the Chicago Temple of the Sons of Liberty, and one of those who brought the "Butternuts" to Chicago "to vote and to fight."

maintain themselves in their respective neighborhoods, districts, States, etc., were to seize upon all the railroads and public buildings, and in the event they were not strong enough to hold all the country, they were to rally around the liberated rebels and their friends at Chicago, Camp Chase, Camp Morton, and other places, after destroying all the public works, railroads, etc., that would be of any service to the Government, in following them up, or baulking their movements. In the meantime, however, the military authorities in Chicago had not been idle, and the rebels and their abettors looked with dismay upon every fresh arrival of troops and artillery, as it was reported in their headquarters by spies, who had the temerity to go to the observatory just opposite the camp, from which they could see almost all over it, and send up hourly reports of everything taking place inside.

They not only had their spies, one might almost say, in Camp Douglas, but in the telegraph offices, and were in or so near Post Headquarters, that they were able to chronicle nearly every event of any importance to them, that transpired, in any of those places.

On the third day of the Convention, it was announced from rebel headquarters at the Richmond House, that the expedition was a failure, that owing to the precautions taken by the military authorities, and the non-arrival of a thousand or two of other Copperheads, who had promised to be in Chicago, ready to assist in the undertaking, and owing to the want of sufficient discipline and organization among the Copperheads, who were on hand, that an attempt at that time upon the garrison of Camp Douglas would involve the destruction of the lives of too many prisoners, and perhaps the killing and capturing of all those who made the attempt to release them. As soon as it was generally known among the rebels that they had failed in attaining the objects for which they came to Chicago, Col. Grenfell and Capt. Castleman made their appearance among them, and stated that it had been generally agreed upon that all who were willing should go to Southern Illinois and Indiana, to drill and organize the Copperheads for the coming struggle, which they thought would take place very soon, or in other words, as soon as Gen. Lee should have Gen. Grant's army in full retreat towards Washington city, or should have inflicted some other almost irreparable disaster upon the Union arms, which event both they and the Copperheads with them, were not only wishing to take place, but confidently expecting every day; that they with Hines and others were going home with some delegates to the Convention, where they could live quietly and work to a great advantage.

On the fourth day of the Convention, the men and officers were paid various sums from twenty to one hundred dollars, and it was left to their option whether they would go to Southern Illinois, Indiana, or return to Canada. Some fifteen or twenty went to Canada, and about fifty went to Southern Illinois and Indiana. Thus ended the first attempt to release the rebel prisoners of war at Camp Douglas. It was certainly a bold movement, both on the part of the rebels, who exposed themselves to such great risk of suffering a disgraceful and ignominious death, and the citizens who aided them in their nefarious designs. But it seemed that an angel of an all-seeing Providence stretched its protecting wings over the fair city, which was doomed by the rebels and their friends at the North first to see and feel the demoralizing influence of an insurrectionary force. What expression, or what degree of contempt is most appropriate for the citizens connected with these rebel efforts;—persons owing a true and faithful allegiance to the Government, yet aiding and abetting its public enemies, persons who while professing a common fealty with their fellow citizens, would welcome to their homes incendiaries, and incite them to murder and plunder those very fellow citizens, and compel them to suffer all the horrors of a cruel warfare! No epithets that human ingenuity could heap upon them would be too harsh, or too undeserved, no contempt too humiliating for a people so devoid of honesty and all the qualities essential to render them prosperous and happy.

CHAP. XII.

THE SECOND ATTEMPT—HINES IN COMMAND AGAIN—COPPERHEADS AGAIN TO BE THE MAIN FORCES TO BE RELIED UPON—REBEL GENERALS TO TAKE COMMAND OF THE RELEASED PRISONERS AND THE INSURRECTIONARY FORCES—THE DAY OF THE PRESIDENTIAL ELECTION APPOINTED AS THE ONE MOST PROPER FOR THE UPRISING—THE CAPTURE OF SOME OF THE REBEL LEADERS AND THEIR SYMPATHIZING FRIENDS.

At the time the rebel officers and soldiers left Chicago, after the Convention, none of them had any idea of ever coming back again, except Capt. Hines and a few of the leaders who consulted with him. He was shrewd enough to see that any effort at that time would be fruitless, and determined, so far as possible, to have all the Copperheads who would assist him in any second affair of the kind, drilled and organized, and men able to render effective assistance. It was for this purpose that he, with his comrades, went to Southern Illinois and Indiana with cavalry and infantry tactics and all the appliances for instructing others in military matters.

The conspirators having failed at Chicago during the convention to make their starting point, having failed to make the great bonfire, which was to be the signal for thousands of others not quite so large, to burn up brightly from almost every hill-top in Ohio, Missouri, Kentucky, Indiana and Illinois, it was necessary for their leaders to meet again, and determine upon a new programme. It appears that they did meet again, and again the starting-point of the whole conspiracy was the release of the rebel prisoners of war at Chicago, and from facts brought to light by the evidence before the great military commission held in Cincinnati, Ohio, the plan of operations was nearly the same as that of the first. The prisoners being released at Chicago, those at Johnston's Island, Camp Morton, Camp Chase and other places were to be released by their friends, and then all were to be immediately placed under the command of rebel generals sent here for the purpose of heading the rebellion, when it once broke out. This may seem like fiction to some; the idea of rebel generals being here in the North for the purpose of aiding and taking the lead of the conspirators; but it is nevertheless true, as disclosed by one of the prisoners taken at Chicago; and it also appears that these generals had several states partitioned off into districts and departments, of which, each department commander was to have exclusive control.

The new programme having been adopted, all that was necessary was to fix upon the day. The day must be one upon which more than the usual number of visitors would be in the city, in order that their coming and staying would not be noticed, and it seemed they selected the day of election, as the one most suitable for their purposes; and if possible a day when the military and civil authorities would be most likely to be caught off their guard. For several days before the 8th of November last, their spies had been coming into the city, in order to get suitable quarters for the men when they arrived, and in parts of the city where they would be least liable to suspicion. In the efforts to secure suitable boarding houses for these incendiaries, various citizens of Chicago took an active part, and even went to the depots to receive them, and escort them into the bosom of the city they were so soon to attempt to destroy. It was not until the Saturday just before the election, that Gen. Sweet had positive information of the *rebels* being in the city, and received full information of the details of their plans, and began to take measures quietly to capture them. This he did at once, and at the same time had every preparation made to repel any attack upon the garrison of Camp Douglas; and he succeeded admirably, following up his information with such energy, that before daylight of the Monday morning following, he had captured enough of the rebel leaders (and their friends in such connexion as to leave no doubt of their guilt,) to make every disloyal man quake in his boots. The captures of the military and police were not confined alone to the conspirators, and in addition to them were captured immense military stores of all kinds, boxes of guns already shotted, cart loads of army pistols loaded and ready for the bloody work expected of them, holsters, pistol belts, cartridges by the cart load, and enough munitions of war to have started an arsenal of moderate size.

These arms were not taken from the rebels, but found in the houses of citizens of Chicago, who can produce witnesses upon the stand (of pretended loyalty and standing, some of them being office-holders under the Government,) to swear that they themselves are, and have always been loyal and true to their allegiance. In the house of Charles Walsh, most of these arms were taken, and also there were captured two rebel soldiers, Captain George Cantrill and Charles Travis Daniels, who were shortly after identified; and Cantrill partly confessed his views, and his complicity with the Copperheads. This man Cantrill had been one of those who had come to Chicago during the Convention, for the same purpose, and averred that then and at the election, the Copperheads had offered and held out to them every inducement to get them here. That had it not been for them he would never have come here. It may be well here to publish a little incident, showing fully the kindred feelings existing between the conspirators and the inmates of Camp Douglas. It was a well known fact, that there were several thousand of John Morgan's desperadoes confined in this prison, and the Copperhead conspirators, to show their refinement of feeling, their accommodating dispositions, and their attention to the worst of these men, had purchased for their use exclusively, the finest cavalry carbines then made in the United States, and had them stored in the immediate neighborhood of the prison, when upon being released they could at once begin to revel in a carnival of blood.

Happy, happy for the people of Chicago, having passed through one of the most critical periods of their existence, without knowing that they were threatened with any disaster, ignorant that there was a mine beneath their feet, just ready to be sprung at any moment, with their own fellow citizens pulling at the spring, willing to involve them in general and complete ruin—willing to subject them to the ravages of such bloodthirsty villains as the inmates of Camp Douglas. The people of Chicago never can appreciate, to its fullest extent, the danger through which they have passed, for several reasons. First, because they were ignorant of it at the time, and the conspirators had and have now at their command, a bitter partizan press in their interests, and entirely subservient to their views, whose interests it is to prevent these facts from becoming generally believed, and when they are presented to the public with the naked truth, to hiss at and cry them down as emanating from the brains of lunatics, or a conspiracy of detectives to ruin the reputation of innocent and guiltless persons. Secondly, because they never experienced the horrors which must necessarily have followed had the conspirators been successful.

CHAP. XIII.

FIRST ATTEMPT OF THE REBELS TO CAPTURE UNITED STATES STEAMER MICHIGAN CARRYING EIGHTEEN GUNS—MODUS OPERANDI—WHY THEY FAILED, &C., &C.—UNITED STATES COMMERCE UPON THE LAKES TO BE DESTROYED—NORTHERN CITIES TO BE LAID UNDER CONTRIBUTION, &C.

Canada, occupying the geographical position and belonging to another nation as it does, has been ever since this war broke out, the rendezvous of thousands upon thousands of the vagabond and criminal population of the United States, together with the rebels and refugees, until its population far exceeds what it had in 1860 ; almost every business occupation is crowded to such an extent that it is almost impossible to obtain employment of any kind, many persons being obliged to keep from starving by begging, for their food, and the clothes they wear upon their backs. Some of this refugee population have means, others are supplied by their friends and families at home ; but by far the greater number are without any occupation or visible means of support, habitué of the gambling hells, drinking saloons, &c., in favor of any crime or villainy to supply their depleted purses, and furnish them with the means of living at ease and idleness. Under such circumstances and among such a class of population, is it anything strange, that the robbery of banks, the pillaging of the inhabitants of the Northern border, that raids with all the necessary plundering and so forth, found plenty of advocates and supporters, and when the time arrived to carry them into execution, plenty of desperadoes, fit tools for such infamous projects. The great difficulty in Canada was not in getting enough of these men to participate in matters of this kind ; but to prevent too many of them from knowing of them, so that there would be a smaller number among whom to divide the spoils and plunder thus obtained, so that the chief difficulty lay in getting together just enough of the most desperate characters to carry out an expedition. During the Chicago Democratic Convention the efforts of the rebels were not confined alone to Camp Douglas ; but simultaneously with their efforts in Chicago, they were to make an attempt to capture the United States Steamer Michigan, carrying eighteen guns, stationed on Lake Erie, the steamer permitted by the treaty between the United States and Great Britain, for the better protection of rebel prisoners confined at Johnston's Island.

The prisoners of war at Chicago, Illinois, being released, and the great conspiracy in the North once fairly inaugurated, the capture of the steamer Michigan was to be one of the combined movements that were to startle the country, and aid the conspiracy in overturning the authority of the United States Government. With the "Michigan" in their hands, the conspirators would have a powerful auxilliary in their pernicious designs upon the country, and be able to render effective aid to the Southern Rebellion; ruining the commercial status of the United States on the great lakes, and effectually closing all the ports on their borders, and in addition to this, their laying all the large towns and cities on the northern portion under contributions, and exacting from them enormous sums of money, through fear of bombardment.

The plan of the conspirators to get possession of the Michigan was by bribery and by surprise. Mr. Thompson, in his efforts to seize the vessel, secured the services of a man named Cole, of Sandusky City, who, whilom, had been a citizen of Virginia, but who still retained his sympathies for the rebellion, and took an active part in aiding it whenever he had an opportunity, and a woman, said to have been his paramour, who carried dispatches backwards and forwards between the parties. This man Cole seems to have been the most wiley conspirator of them all, and played his infamous part of the plot with the most adroit shrewdness; and the defeat of the whole scheme was not owing to any blunder of his, but rather the blunder of those who employed and furnished him with the means.

Having been well supplied with money by Mr. Thompson, and no limit put to his expenses, he began his work with a will. He seems to have begun by getting generally well acquainted with the officers of the vessel, by feasting them, and now and then lending them money, or accommodating them in some other way, until he had won the confidence of all those in command of the steamer, as well as those in charge of Johnston's Island. After a time, he found out those who were most vulnerable on the money question, and those whom he did not dare to approach upon the subject. Of the latter class, there is one mentioned in particular by the rebels, whose suspicions they did not care to arouse, and which they made every attempt to lull. This was an officer named Eddy, from Massachusetts. Of the former class, whom they bribed, the rebels mentioned particularly the chief engineer, who, they said, had agreed, for twenty thousand dollars in gold, to get the machinery out of order, and otherwise aid in the vessel's capture, and one or two others.

Of the remainder of the officers of the Michigan, they thought their well-known Democratic faith and sympathy with the rebellion, would prevent them from seeing or knowing *too much*, until too late to avoid the disaster. Of these last, the conspirators did not seem to entertain the least fear, some of them being Southern men by birth, and at most, but passive in their fidelity to the government. The men of the vessel who were loyal, were also tampered with, and the rebels in Canada looked for assistance from them, and claimed that some of their own men from Canada had enlisted on board of her for the purpose of aiding to capture her. Of these rebels, however, there were but few. As the writer has stated before, the attempt on the steamer Michigan was to be simultaneous with that at

BRIG. GEN. CHARLES WALSH,

A citizen of Chicago, he was at one time the Democratic candidate for Sheriff of Cook County, in which is the city of Chicago, during the earliest part of the war he was very active in helping to raise what was called the Irish brigade. He afterwards became a bitter democratic partizan and was connected with the Sons of Liberty. Just before and during the Convention he received into his family several rebel soldiers who were there during the day and night time, making cartridges for the expected release of the rebel prisoners of war at Camp Douglas. He was arrested in his own house on the morning of the 7th of November, as was also his son, and two Rebel soldiers and taken to Camp Douglas. In his house and on his premises were an immense numbers of guns of several kinds and also immense military stores, consisting of powder, buckshot, cartridges, with two or three cast braces of army revolvers, all these guns and pistols were loaded and ready with the exception of being capped. Charles Walsh is of Irish extraction and about forty years of age, and a fine looking man. He is generous, impulsive, rather easily influenced, agreeable in conversation, and except in the character he assumed as an enemy to his country was possessed of qualities which would win for him many friends. There are as bad men, in our opinion, as Mr. Charles Walsh, to day at liberty and talking treason in our midst.

Chicago, Ill., and while the rebels and their friends were assembling in Chicago, they were also gathering in Sandusky City, for the capture of the Michigan. The exact number of conspirators in Sandusky, at that time, is not known to the writer, nor the details of their plans; but let it suffice to say, *that they were there, armed and ready.* When the time of action arrived, however, the engineer and his accomplices were no where to be found, and after waiting for nearly two days, the rebel portion of the conspirators, with the exception of Capt. Beall, returned to Canada. On their return, they said that the persons whom they had bribed were afraid to toe the mark—that is, were afraid to carry out their infamous and hazardous part of the contract.

The rebels were in great fear, lest something had happened that would put an end forever to their hopes, in regard to the steamer, but in a few days after this, the non-appearance of the engineer and friends, were duly explained, and the alarm caused by it quieted, and another time set for the attempt; the sequel will show how *much* they intended, and how much they ventured to effect their aims. It is a well known fact that the rebels while in Sandusky city, were feasted and toasted in the houses of some of the prominent citizens and business men, and encouraged in every way by them. The day being set once more, preparations were again made to capture the vessel, and this time occurred what was called the *Lake Erie Piracy*, nearly everything connected with which was so disgraceful to the United States service, that although the government hastened to remove all the reprehensible officers, and retain those who deserved well of their country, yet seems to have endeavored to keep some of the facts connected with it, from being made public. About one week before the time set for the second attempt arrived, Capt. Beall returned from Sandusky to Windsor, Canada West, and announced that all was ready for the capture, and immediately telegraphed to Jacob Thompson, who was then at the Queen's Hotel, in Toronto, who at once answered that he would come to Windsor that night, and desired not to be recognized. That evening he arrived at Windsor, and without apparently being known got into a carriage waiting, and was taken to the residence of a Col. Steele, about a mile below Windsor, where he was expected. During this week all the men who were to participate in the affair were notified, and this time the services of some of the men who had been to Chicago during the Convention, were called into requisition. The officers of the rebel army could be seen running about, here and there, to the different boarding houses where the men were stopping, carrying ominous looking carpet bags, distributing from them pistols, ammunition and other things, deemed necessary for the undertaking, which was to be made on the night of the following Monday. Most active in these efforts to incite these men to deeds of desperation, were Col. Steele and Jake Thompson—or when he used his assumed name, Col. Carson.

The plans of the pirates were as follows, and the writer gives them just as he heard them from the lips of two of the rebel officers who participated in the affair, commanding detachments on board of the "Philo Parsons." Part of the men, amounting in all to about seventy-five, were to go from Canada to Sandusky city by rail, another party were to cross the river at Detroit early on Monday morning, and take passage on the steamer "Philo Parsons" for Sandusky, another portion were to take passage on her from Sandwich, Canada, about two miles below Detroit, and still another party of them, consisting of about fifteen (with eight or ten citizens who knew nothing of what was contemplated), on Sunday morning were to charter a small steamer called the "Scotia," plying between Windsor and Detroit, ostensibly for the purpose of taking a pleasure ride to Malden, Canada, about twenty miles below Detroit, and near the entrance of the river into the lake, when they were also on Monday to take passage for the same place on the Parsons. At Kelley's Island, one of the points at which the boat touched in her daily trips, they were to receive a messenger from Cole, letting them know, that up to that time everything was going on smoothly in Sandusky; upon receiving this information, all the different portions of the gang were to unite and seize the steamer, before she reached the next landing, at which she generally stopped. The engineers and pilots were to be forced, by threats of instant death if they refused, to still occupy their respective places; the passengers were to be put off at some out of the way place, where it would be impossible for them to give any information to the authorities, and after dark they were to run down into Sandusky bay, where they would see certain signals, made by those conspirators on the shore, when they would land, take on board all those who had come by rail from Detroit, and some Copperheads from Cincinnati, Ohio, and other places, and at once would immediately turn the prow of the Parson for the steamer Michigan. Cole was to give a champagne supper on board the Michigan that evening, to the officers, and was to be there himself with a party of rebels, who had also become well acquainted with the officers, and was invited at the request of Cole, to join in the festivities of the occasion. It was intended for the Philo Parsons to reach hailing distance of the Michigan about eleven or twelve o'clock that night, in order that by this time as many of the crew as possible, through the champagne, would be incapable of rendering any resistance, when the Parson was hailed by the watch on board the steamer, and Cole and his associates were at once to take possession of a gun, which would sweep the whole decks, to prevent that portion of the crew who were not rendered incapable of it by drink, from attempting any effectual resistance to the conspirators boarding her from the Parsons. Once in possession of this vessel of war, the prisoners on the island were to be immediately released, landed at Sandusky, when the Sons of Liberty, Illini and other secret societies were to seize the opportunity of rising up, and asserting their peculiar doctrines, under the protection of this powerful man of war. The same course was to be pursued at Cleveland and other places, along the lake coast, where their secret societies were in full blast, the conspirators exacting an enormous tribute of the loyal portion of these communities to save their property from the dangers of bombardment. This expected tribute of ten millions of dollars, (to be divided equally among them,) from the border cities, was the greatest inducement held out by the rebel leaders before leaving Canada, to their desperadoes, in order to excite their cupidity and zeal, and inflame their minds to such a pitch, that they would render a strict obedience to their officers, and hesitate at no act of violence.

These were the plans of the conspirators, and although they may seem almost ideal and improbable, yet are very possible even to the most minute details, when one will take time to stop and consider the great chances of success the pirates had in having a portion of the crew bribed, and their prospects of having the remainder too excited by liquor, to make any effectual opposition—the surprise, the chaos and confusion of the crew at finding those whom they supposed their friends, as well as their own comrades and fellow-soldiers, fighting them hand to hand.

Under such circumstances as these, it is very easy to conceive of the capture of a vessel by a band of desperadoes, who would hesitate at no act of bloodshed or villainy to accomplish their objects. In addition to this, they were rendered more desperate, if such a thing could be, by the certainty that if they failed and were captured, a speedy and disgraceful death awaited them.

The Michigan being captured, it is also easy to conceive that all the other portions of their plans could have been carried out, perhaps to a greater extent than already mentioned, that contributions could have been levied and exacted from the people, and especially that the Sons of Liberty and other secret societies would joyously seize such an opportunity as the protection of this man-of-war afforded them, to throw off the mantle of secrecy and darkness from their hell-born principles, and parade them to the view of the public in all their hideousness.

We will now follow up the plans of the conspirators, and mention the facts as they occurred. On Sunday the —tn of September, just preceding the attempt, although it was a rainy and very disagreeable day, in accordance with orders, the Scotia was chartered and conveyed her part of the pirates, together with some arms to Malden, C. W. It is due to the citizens who were with the pirates, to say here, that they had no idea that the piracy was contemplated, and thought that it was only a fishing excursion, which at that time was a very common occurrence with the Southeners at Windsor.

That evening when the Scotia returned, they alleged that it was so unpleasant that they would wait until the next day before going back to Windsor, in this way lulling everything like suspicion in the minds of those who had only been invited to go with them, the more effectually to conceal the real objects of the pirates. On Monday, on the arrival of the Steamer *Philo Parsons* at Malden, those who had taken passage from Detroit and Sandwich, were seen in very conspicuous places on the decks, by those on the wharf, who immediately boarded her in the capacity of passengers. It was not the intention of the pirates to seize the vessel until nearly to Sandusky, and in the event they received no messenger from *Cole*, at Kelley's's Island, they were not to take possession of her at all, but continue in their characters as passengers to Sandusky, and there learn the cause of his failure to communicate with them. But as subsequent events will show, they were compelled to change their whole plan of operations. Shortly after the vessel left Malden, the frequency with which all of these men patronized the bar of the boat, attracted the suspicious of some of the passengers, as well as the officers, one of whom, from some remarks let fall by one of the men, thought they were a suspicious set, and said that as soon as the boat arrived at Sandusky, he would have them arrested and taken care of. Some of the pirates happened to hear this remark, and as soon as it was generally known, created the greatest consternation among them, and upon arriving at Kelley's Island and not receiving the messenger promised by *Cole*, they were in a very unenviable position. To go to Sandusky they would be arrested; the only course they could take to save their own lives and liberty, was that which they eventually adopted.

Capt. Beall, after hearing this report, quickly determined to seize the vessel, which was accordingly done, to the great terror of the passengers and crew. One or two of the crew who refused to obey the orders given by the pirates, were severely wounded. Finding that there was only wood enough on board to last for a short time, she was run to Put-in-bay to get a supply, and it was at this landing that they seized the Island Queen, which happened to be there also, for the same purpose. This vessel, after removing her valuables, was immediately scuttled and left floating with the current in a sinking condition. After dark that night, the pirates ran down into Sandusky Bay, but failing to see the signals agreed upon, and after waiting a short time, again returned to the open lake, convinced by this time that something had happened to their friends in Sandusky. Capt. Beall then seeing that something had happened which would prevent them from capturing the Michigan, announced his determination to cruise on the lake as long as possible, burning and destroying all he could, and endeavored to induce his men to go with him; but they were already scared, and begun to fear the consequences of their act, and insisted upon going back to Canada. This is what Capt. Beall himself told Mr. Thompson on his return to Canada, that " if it had not been for these mutinous scoundrels, I could have run that boat on these lakes for two weeks, burning and destroying all the vessels we met with, before the Yankees could have made us take to land."

The owners of shipping upon the great lakes, can now if they never could before, appreciate fully the danger to their vessels at that time. The day before the rebels left Windsor, C. W., the United States authorities had been notified of the expedition, and fully placed upon their guard, and if the plans of Lieut. Col. Hill, the efficient commander of the post at Detroit could have been followed, he would have captured the whole gang. However, he telegraphed to Sandusky, and had Cole arrested while he was sitting at the table, taking dinner with the officers on board the Michigan. This effectually prevented Cole from communicating with the conspirators. Col. Hill's plans were to let the pirates take the *Parsons*, and then before they had time to do any damage, have the Michigan meet them on their way to Sandusky and capture them all together, and thus releive the Government from any farther trouble with this most desperate band of incendaries. Col. Hill telegraphed to the commander of the Michigan, requesting him to do this, and it is generally understood that the reason why he did not do it was that the machinery of the vessel was out of order, thus showing how well those who had been bribed had done their duty.

In addition to these attempts to capture the steamer Michigan, was the celebrated St. Albans raid, which among others, was one of the rebel modes of carrying the war into Africa and harrassing the northern border.

This raid, which has become so famous in the history of this war, was first started by a Texan, named *Bracey*, belonging to one of the rebel Texan regiments. This man, for four or five years before the war, had been going to one of the schools or colleges (according to his own account of himself,) in St. Albans, and was well acquainted, both with the city and country, in the immediate neighborhood. He gave all the information he could, and offered to return there to get more, which he, with one or two rebel soldiers did, and obtained all the necessary information that would, in any way, aid them in their criminal designs. Upon their report, on their return to Canada, the fitting out the expedition immediately began—the money, arms, etc., being furnished by the rebel agents in Montreal or Quebec. Of the details of this affair, as carried out, the people have been fully advised by the newspapers, and, to all intents and purposes, the raid has been a success, or has operated in this manner by the winding and twisting course of the Canadian law courts, which seem to be actuated by no fixed principles, but wavering between the fear of the public opinion of the American people, and their desire to aid the rebels in overturning the government—and had it not been for the sudden turn the war has taken in the last six months, the people along the northern border would have been subjected to numerous other and similar raids. The St. Albans raid was only a part of one grand scheme of the rebels, for the past two years, to inaugurate a new mode of warfare, entirely beyond the pale of that waged by civilized nations, and a relic of the more barbarous ages. This new mode of warfare, or incendiarism, as it is generally called, was first started by the rebel government, after the fall of Memphis, Tenn., for the purpose of destroying vessels, loaded with government property, and cut off the communications of the armies in the lower countries, with their depots of supplies; with this end in view, companies of men were regularly enlisted for the purpose, and after a time, the sympathies and the aid rendered the rebellion by certain classes of the people at the North, justified them in extending its pernicious effects further North. Companies were enlisted and sent through the lines, with orders to burn public buildings, army stores, and supplies, wherever they could find them. Thus far, secret agents of the rebels were scattered all over the North, in small squads, wherever there was a prospect of doing injury to the government; and it is to the efforts of these men, that the country is indebted for the wholesale destruction of steamboat and other property at St. Louis, Cairo, and other places on the western rivers. These men performing the incendiary acts frequently upon information furnished them by their sympathizing friends. The public are already well aware of the manner in which some of these acts of incendiarism terminated, most especially the attempt of Capt. Kennedy and others, holding commissions in the rebel service, to burn New York city. If ever a man deserved his fate, this man Kennedy certainly did, and the public, having been saved, unscathed, can never fully appreciate the enormity of his crime. One, knowing the facts of these men being in the North for this purpose, can readily appreciate the punishment awarded them; but upon reviewing all the facts in the case, will as readily say that they are now less guilty than the citizens of the North, who aided them in their designs, by furnishing them information and associating with them, and even receiving them into their families, while they were yet public enemies, and in arms against the country.

CHAP. XIV.

SABBATH EVENING IN INVINCIBLE CLUB HALL.—A SCENE NEVER TO BE FORGOTTEN—PLANS REHEARSED—ARMS INSPECTED—REPORT OF THE BRIG.-GEN. OF THE SONS OF LIBERTY—REVOLUTION AND BLOODSHED WITHIN THE NEXT THIRTY-SIX HOURS—DISTRIBUTION OF FIREARMS UPON OUR STREETS.

The evening of the 3d of November, 1864, found a large representation of the Sons of Liberty in their lodge room in Chicago, for as the time drew near for the Presidential election—the period fixed for the carnival of crime—the members of the organization realized the importance of the utmost vigilance—lest their plans should be discovered—and of the most entire concurrence with their leaders, and concert of action in obeying the commands that might be given. At this meeting, the Brigadier-General of the Order was present, as were also Captains and Lieutenants of the Invincible Club, and a more exciting meeting had rarely ever been held in the Temple. Speakers were vehement and earnest, and their theme was the proposed uprising. As had ever been their policy, certain important facts were withheld from the fledglings in treason, who had not yet tried their wings, but there was no discord, no dissention, and all exhibited enthusiasm and confidence. Brig.-Gen. Walsh called a meeting of the Order, to be held in the hall of the Invincible Club, on Sunday evening November 6th, the hour being fixed for eight o'clock. All were exhorted to be "on hand," as the Brig.-General had an important communication to make.

Friday and Saturday an immense number of pistols, and much ammunition were sold, and many were given away in quarters, where it was certain material aid might be expected, when the time should arrive for the inauguration of revolution. To the few of us having the interests of the country at heart, who were cognisant of the acts, preparations and intentions of the Order, it will readily be believed the days were tedious, and the nights sleepless. So well had the principal secrets of the Order—the details of the uprising—been kept from the lower degree of the "Sons," that but few of the members had a definite idea of the infamous part they were expected to perform, and it was to communicate enough information to secure harmony among the men, and that concert of action which promised the most complete success of the terrible scheme of villainy before them, that the meeting was called for Sabbath evening. It will be seen by the report of

Gen. Sweet's testimony, before the military commission, to what peril the city was exposed. With but a handful of men to garrison the post, without the ability to obtain adequate reinforcements, with ten thousand veteran rebels in a camp, so incomplete in its structure, with the certainty that our secret enemies were upon the railroads already, and seeking positions in the post-office, in telegraph offices, if, as there was good reason to apprehend, the telegraph stations were not already under their control, that by Judge Morris' official report to the Temple, two full regiments of Sons of Liberty, all well armed and disciplined, were ready at an hour's notice, and that a third regiment was almost complete, the knowledge also that the entire body of Copperheads in the State, and in the northwest, would rise simultaneously with the traitors in our city, with good reason to believe it impossible to safely communicate with the head of the State military department—in this most enenviable position, to know that the fatal moment was fast coming, when the infernal machinery was to be set in motion, and to make arrangements to avert the catasrophe so quietly as not to arrest attention, or excite the alarm of the leaders of the plot, which would have instantly been executed, had it become apparent that the movements of these traitors were watched; these considerations and the discharge of the fearful responsibilities resting upon the only parties who could then hope to avert the danger, occupied the mind and hands of the commandant of the post, and employed the utmost vigilance of the writer and able assistants. Every few hours orderlies and special couriers were despatched to the headquarters of the camp, with such reports as could be obtained. We have read Eastern tales of travelers, when accident had discovered them in closest proximity to the deadly cobra de capello, the breathless horror with which they contemplated its motions, and saw it slowly coiling itself upon their limbs, or upon a table at their bedsides, and knowing that a single motion on the part of the imperilled person would be but to invite certain death, the vigilance and eager solicitude, the distressing anxiety with which they regarded the movements and intent of the venomous creature, but never till a full realization of our position in regard to this organized band of traitors, did we ever experience sensations akin to those of the unfortunate traveler; and when the loathsome reptile had got into a position where it was safe to attempt its destruction, and when this attempt was successful, no greater relief or deeper emotions of gratitude could have been felt by him—a moment before exposed to instant and terrible death—than were experienced by us when the danger had been averted.

Sunday evening came. Our citizens worshiping in the churches, or in peaceful repose in their own residences, little knew of the imminent peril to which they were exposed, or of the gathering of their fellow citizens in the Invincible Club Hall to arrange the details which, if successful, would bring ruin, desolation and death to thousands of our unsuspecting people. Up the entrance to the hall, cautiously crept the members of the order, peering behind them, and advancing one by one, or in groups of two or three, till they reached the hall. The door was guarded by a sentinel, so that intrusion was out of the question. At nine o'clock, the assemblage was called to order by Obadiah Jackson, Jr., Esq., the Grand Seignior. Patrick Dooley, Secretary, was in his place on the right of the Grand Seignior. The meeting was large, and a more desperate looking collection of men have rarely assembled in a convention in our city. Such desecration of the evening of the Sabbath has never before been witnessed here. After the opening of the meeting, one of the members took early occasion to remark substantially, that it must have been noticed by all present, as well as himself, that the city was full of strangers, and that he had noticed many of them were dressed in butternut clothes, and had good reason to believe that they were Abolitionists in disguise; that it was advisable to watch them, it being his confident opinion that they had come to the city for the purpose of fraudulently voting the Abolition ticket; and the speaker was proceeding in this strain, much to the amusement of the members of the higher degree, to whom the men in butternut clothes were no strangers. The speaker had scarcely taken his seat, when James A. Wilkinson, Past Grand Seignior, rose and stated that the suspicious looking persons were "our friends," and that he himself had brought a company of sixty of them to the city, and that they were entitled to every attention, as they would do good service for "us," and stated that he was going back for more.

The strangers who were the subject of discussion, were from the counties in the Southern part of the State, and all bore the same general appearance of vagabonds, cut-throats, felons, bounty-jumpers and deserters. They had all seemed to appear simultaneously in our city, unheralded even to the "Sons," and their advent was as much a subject of remark, as would have been a shower of toads and tadpoles. They did not take up their quarters at respectable hotels and private houses, but sneaked away stealthily to the lowest dens of vice, and resorts of criminals unwhipped of justice. They came to help perform infamous work, and had a part of the price of their guilt upon their persons, or had already invested it for the poorest quality of intoxicating liquors. They had been collected together from the various country towns in the Southern part of the State, where they had been in training under the command of rebel officers, and many of them were the same parties who had come to Chicago at the time of the Democratic National Convention, hopeful and confident of the uprising, and who had been so wofully disappointed, and turned their backs so reluctantly upon our banks and stores, from which they had intended to glut their avarice, and amply remunerate themselves with the property of our citizens. Nothing on earth is more positively certain than, had the work not been arrested at the moment it was, these devils would have pillaged every bank and rifled every storehouse in Chicago; and it is equally certain that beyond Colonel Sweet and the writer, with his assistant, Robert Alexander, none knew of the intricate deadly plot in detail, although Major-General Hooker, Brig.-Gen. Paine, Governor Yates, Hon. I. N. Arnold, and William Rand, Esq., of the *Tribune*, had been informed by the writer of the general intent of the organization.

But to return to the secret convention at the hall. The explanation of J. A. Wilkinson not being satisfactory to Mr. Hull, some curt remarks were banded between the speakers, which Obadiah Jackson, Jr., Esq., the Grand Seignior could not well control, Brig.-Gen. Charlie Walsh rose to his feet and said unhesitatingly, that he had by his own order " brought these men here to *vote and to fight*," and he added, " by God they will vote early and often, and they will fight." Gen. Walsh desired that all the " brethren" would extend the hospitalities of the city to the visitors, for they were " our friends." While this discussion was going on, there was a Confederate officer in the hall, and within ten feet of Walsh. The joy upon the announcement by Walsh, found expression in a rude and boisterous manner. It having been definitely settled that the wretches who had been the subject of discussion were good for any number of votes, and fully prepared to take part in the attack, so soon to startle our city; the convention proceeded to ascertain who among its members were unarmed, and to supply such delinquents forthwith. The members generally exhibited revolvers of various patterns, but upon inspection by the officers, preference was expressed for the pattern like those which were subsequently found in the house of Walsh, by the officers, at the time of his arrest. There were several who had not the approved pattern, and such persons were instructed to apply next morning at the store of James Geary, corner of Wells and Madison streets, and they would be supplied, but upon consultation it was remarked by Geary, that as he was already suspected he feared it would hardly be expedient for Walsh to send arms to him for distribution, and it was agreed by J. H. Hubbard, the treasurer of the Invincible Club, that he would receive possession of the revolvers, and give them to all who might apply, and such persons were to call at the door of the Invincible Club hall, at 9 o'clock the next morning, when they would be supplied. It was arranged that a guard of not less than fifty or one hundred men, all well armed, should remain all day on Tuesday, (election day,) at the polls in each ward, making not *less* than one full regiment in the aggregate, thus detailed for special " service."

To distinguish friends and members at a time when trouble should break out, was a subject now raised for debate, and it was finally agreed that the members should wear McClellan badges upon the left breast, attached by *red and white* ribbons. It was understood that orderlies were to be constantly reporting from each ward at the headquarters of Gen. Walsh, and thus a regular line of communication would be kept up, which in case of trouble, would be greatly to the advantage of these ruffians. They were all advised to deposit their vote with one hand, and present their revolver with the other. It was confidently asserted by individuals, but with how much truth we know not, that an Invincible Club from Philadelphia, would also be present and help do the voting, but as no Philadelphia Roughs were reported in the city, the help expected from Philadelphia probably did not arrive. The most violent secession speeches were made by Duncan, who was then connected with the Mercantile agency in McCormick's block, Walsh, Wilkinson, and many others.

The meeting adjourned at a late hour, and many of the leaders, prominent among whom was James Geary, proceeded to a secure retreat, and then in the quiet hours of Sunday night, gave away a great number of revolvers of the same style and pattern with those subsequently siezed by the authorities.

CHAP. XV.

ARRESTS—GREAT EXCITEMENT—GENERAL CONSTERNATION OF THE COPPERHEADS—NEW VICTORIES IN THE FIELD—DEATH-BLOW OF JEFF. DAVIS' SECRET ORGANIZATION AND HOPES IN THE NORTH—FINDING OF ARMS—THE EFFECT ALL THROUGHOUT THE NORTH-WEST.

Before the morning of Monday, November 7th dawned, a dispatch, embracing the most important features of the Sunday night meeting, had been prepared by the writer, and forwarded to the commandant of Camp Douglas, who, during the night, arrested Judge Morris, Brig.-Gen. Charles Walsh, and others, and a large number of "butternuts," who had been the subject of discussion at the Sunday night meeting, and these prisoners were safely lodged in Camp Douglas. The news of the arrests, and the charges upon which they were made, caused intense excitement among all classes, loyal men rejoicing for the promptness and wisdom of the measure, while the Copperheads howled fearfully, and denounced it as a fresh evidence of "Lincoln's tyranny." As the facts became generally known, there was an unanimous expression of approval on the part of all good, loyal citizens. The consternation of the Copperheads was truly great; they felt that, notwithstanding their many precautions for secrecy, the eye of the government had been upon them in their most secret places, and this consternation was not by any means relieved when they read in the morning papers an extract of Brig.-Gen. Charles Walsh's speech before the order in the Invincible Club hall. They felt certain that they were watched, and that they were under careful espionage, and the effect was precisely what we had expected and desired. It was telegraphed in every direction, that the government had a complete knowledge of their designs and proceedings, and such a tremor and quaking with fear the Copperheads had not previously exhibited. It completely deranged their designs, and caused an utter abandonment of the plot, for the leaders in Chicago having been arrested, no one knew how soon his turn would come, and it is a general and well-established fact, that however sanguinary and fiendish a rabble may prove when attacking their victims by surprise, the mass of such beings lose their brute courage when discovering, to a certainty, that the details of their strategy are known, and the party upon whom an assault is contemplated is prepared, and will repel the attack with that fury, vigor, desperation and perseverance that will surely carry death to many of the assailants. They lack zeal, because they know their cause is a bad one, just as one honest man will put three rogues to flight. It was telegraphed that the heads of the government were fully advised of the conspiracy, and that officers were freely visiting all the more important temples in the North-West, mingling in the "business" of these meetings, and apprising the military leaders of every move which had been made, which was being made, and which was contemplated. Suspicion was aroused, and so general did this distrust soon become, that no one was willing to trust his neck in a halter, and any one of his associates having possession of the other end. Suddenly a most wonderful reform was apparent, as rats disappear from view after a few have been captured. Those who were at Invincible Club hall, and made secession speeches, declared they were all drunk, or were not in earnest, and other equally flimsy excuses;—these are the apologies members made to each other, presuming they were addressing the party who had surrendered them to the government. It was amusing to notice their trepidation. They were variously affected. Capt. P. D. Parks, of the Invincible Club, really cried, like a whipped schoolboy, from fear; many ran away with all possible speed. Doolittle, the man of valor, who was to lead a party against Camp Douglas, was the first to run away, and from certain "surface indications," we rather think he is running yet. James A. Wilkinson, the valorous Past Grand Seignior, has gone to look after Doolittle; Silver has gone to Canada; Strawn has turned a summerset into the Republican party; S. Corning Judd helped to convict the prisoners in Cincinnati, although called by the defense; Amos Green, the Major-General of the Order in Illinois, has quietly subsided, and is no longer belligerent; Vallandigham gives the Order the cold-shoulder, and affects pious horror upon the recital of its aims and purposes—and, indeed, the whole organization, as formidable as it was in numbers, was soon in the most terrible condition, and died in great agony. The complications of the disease of which the order came to its death, would puzzle the most profound pathologist. It might, perhaps, be set down as a disease of the heart, induced by corrupt morals, with the following complications: Softening of the brain from the study of State sovereignty; extreme nervous debility from the reproach of a guilty conscience; injury to the spine by suddenness of fall; weakness of the limbs from bad whiskey, and impurity of the blood from contamination. The child of secession is dead—as dead as the cause of the Southern Confederacy! Jeff. Davis' pet institution was decently buried within the enclosure of Camp Douglas. There being no provision or service in the ritual for this occasion, we may only exclaim, as we look upon his last resting-place, "*Requiescat in pace.*"

The arrest of General Walsh and others, and the discovery of a great number of revolvers, etc., all loaded and ready for use, and the rather unpleasant discovery that the Brigadier-General had actually employed a Government detective to go to his house and give instructions in making cartridges, were *rather* mortifying to the order, and when it appeared that the Chairman of the Vigilance Committee, whose province was to take the balance of the arms, which we learned were in

Walsh's barn, and with all possible haste remove them to a place of safety, and the Chairman (who makes this record for the edification of his constituents), deemed the safest place he could find the retired locality of Camp Douglas, and if the inquisitive eyes of Gen. Sweet, and his grasping propensities, should take possession of all the valuable carbines, Enfield rifles, muskets and revolvers, let them moderate their wrath, and find consolation in the thought that in their last hour it will be a pleasant reflection that all those bristling warlike implements fell into the hands of men who will not put them to base uses.

When it was announced, with all confidence, that beneath the hay in Charley Walsh's barn was a large number of firearms that must be speedily removed, a new idea of the value of ladies' hoops burst upon the world (not "The Wide-Wide World,") but the few who were present when James L. Rock, one of the editors of the Chicago *Times* announced that his wife (and Mr. Rock ought to know), and some other ladies could quickly remove these weapons by concealing them under their hoops, Colonel Sweet, with his usual gallantry, spared the ladies the inconvenience and trouble, and removed them quite as well and as quickly.

After the first arrests, other followed, but after a time many of these worthies were liberated, not because of their innocence; and they may now one and all consider themselves on their good behavior.

After the first arrests, the hall of the "Temple" in Chicago was deserted. It was not thought to be exactly *safe*, and meetings were held occasionally wherever they could find a place of safety, where it was morally certain Gen. Sweet would not know of their gatherings or of their business, and where it would be a dead secret forever; and they one and all swore that whoever had exposed them to the Government *should die by assassination*. This was their fixed purpose, and when suspicion fastened upon Hull, no less than three persons *volunteered* to do the deed, those men were Lewis C. Morrison, old Felton, the Outside Guardian, and, by his own confession, detective of the order, and James L. Rock, one of the editors o the Chicago *Times*.

Two of these "gentlemen" visited the office of the writer of this book during the progress of the trial, and used the following language. "If it be *true*, (he having inferred from Alexander's testimony that the writer had been in the interest of the General Government), a thousand times you had better be Charley Walsh than Dr. Ayer."

A project was considered to rally the order and carry out the original programme, but as well might an attempt have been made to infuse life into a body that had been buried a fortnight. A messenger who went to Lewiston, Ill., to "see what the order would do about it," were coolly told by their Grand Commander, S. Corning Judd, Esq., that " they would'nt do a thing." This unsatisfactory report proved two things—that S. Corning Judd, Grand Commander, and candidate for Lieut. Governor of Illinois, (who might have got the election, if the " ballot and bullet" butternut machinery had only proved available), considered the institution as "gone up," and 2d—that he was ungrateful to a people who had at least made him their nominee.

Gentlemen who, by request, visited the different sections of the State and of the Northwest, all reported that immediately after it was known that the Government knew their secrets as well as they did themselves, they tacitly agreed not to regard themselves as a "secret" organization in future, and we have the best of reasons to believe the entire order is so completely uprooted that it can never again spring up to curse the land. Home traitors have been taught, and it is well if they profit by the lesson, they cannot form any society or order based upon treason, that can for any considerable time continue "secret." Its purposes will transpire, for the all-seeing eye of Him who reads the hearts of men, and will not suffer "a sparrow to fall to the ground without his notice," that God who hath decreed that this nation shall be re-united, shall be prosperous, free, happy, and truly great, will not suffer traitors to be successful, but will give them into the hands of those who reverence His mighty and terrible name; and their cunning shall be a reproach, and their machinations shall be known of all men, and they shall blush with burning shame that they were ever false to their country.

JUDGE BUCKNER S. MORRIS,

A prominent lawyer and citizen of Chicago, a bitter and strong advocate of Democratic faith and the peculiar notions of the Sons of Liberty. He was arrested at the same time with Walsh in his own house. He was a strong Southern man in his feelings and openly sympathized with the rebellion, and so strong were his sympathies that he frequently furnished escaped rebel prisoners of war with clothing, food, and money, and otherwise aided them in escaping from the country. B. S. Morris was at one time Judge of the Circuit Court of Cook County, and was a candidate for Governor of the State of Illinois. He was born in Kentucky, and is about sixty years of age. Outside of his treason, Judge Morris was generally regarded as possessing many noble qualities of heart.

CHAP. XVI.

TESTIMONY OF GEN. B. J. SWEET—LIST OF OFFICERS AND MEMBERS OF THE McCLELLAN CLUBS IN CHICAGO.

The services of Brig.-Gen. B. J. Sweet, in relation to the Northwestern Conspiracy, have already been briefly mentioned, and the reader will perhaps find the report of that officer's testimony full of interest. After the communications by the writer to Gen. Sweet (then Colonel) in command of Camp Douglas, which were made by request of Gen. Paine, dispatches were regularly forwarded to that officer, who never failed to receive them with gratification. The service was one of extreme danger, difficulty and delicacy, requiring the most careful attention, unceasing vigilance, and only the consciousness of discharging an important and imperative duty to the country, and the confident belief that invaluable aid might thus be rendered, could have induced the writer to enter upon and pursue a line of service, a thousand times more distasteful and perilous than active service upon the field.

The recognition of the writer's services by Brig.-Gen. Paine, and subsequently by Maj. Gen. Hooker, in commendatory letters, will ever be remembered, showing as it did, a grateful appreciation by those gallant officers, of services of which, from their character, the public could have no knowledge for the time being.

The following is the testimony of Gen. Sweet, as substantially given before the military commission in Cincinnati:

EVIDENCE OF COLONEL SWEET.

My name is Benjamin J. Sweet; I am and was, during the months of September, October, and November of last year, Colonel of the 8th Regiment Veteran Reserve Corps; I was also, and still am, Commandant of the Post of Chicago, including Camp Douglas. The post I command extended, I suppose to the limits of the surrounding posts.

The Judge Advocate.—What are the geographical limits of the command of the Post of Chicago.

Mr. Asay objected to the question, as involving a matter of law and not of evidence, but his objection was overruled by the Court.

Witness continued.—My jurisdiction extends to the limits of the posts north at Madison, Wisconsin, southwest to Rock Island, south, or almost south, to Springfield, and east to Detroit, Michigan. The Commandant has jurisdiction over everything pertaining to military affairs in the jurisdiction, over the command of all troops, and for the protection of the property of the Government and of the people. Chicago is one of the first military depots of supplies in the country. There are ten depots in charge of a Colonel, and Chicago is one of them. The Depot Quartermaster at that time was Colonel Potter. From the commencement to the latter end of August, the number of troops under my command, fit for duty, was from 800 to 900. Towards the end of August, I was reinforced by about 1,200 men, consisting of four companies of one hundred days' men, and the 196th Pennsylvania Regiment, which numbered 750 men, also one hundred days' men; these remained with me sixty or seventy days. I telegraphed for these reinforcements. There were between 8,000 and 9,000 prisoners in camp up to November. On the 6th of November, the morning report shows 796 men, rank and file, fit for duty. There were always on duty in Chicago about sixty men acting as provost guard; this left 736 men in camp to do guard duty. The sixty men in the city performed service in looking after deserters, guarding property, &c. The depot for supplies is in the city, and is in charge of the depot quartermaster. Troops were used for doing camp duty, and guarding prisoners of war, and forwarding deserters to various camps. The entire guard in Camp Douglas was about 500 men, 250 on duty at a time, and 250 off. These were changed every other day. The camp is within the city limits, and is about three miles from the Court House.

The conveniences to reach the camp are by way of street cars. There were buildings on the north side of the camp; on the opposite side of the street, also on the east side, there was a hotel and other dwellings. Walsh's house was about one-fourth of a mile from the camp, with three or four houses between Walsh's house and the camp. My duties are twofold; I have to report to Gen. Cook, at Springfield, commanding in the State, and to Gen. Hooker, at Department headquarters. In relation to prisoners of war, I am under the instructions of the Commissary General of prisoners at Washington. These prisoners were arrested at my order. Messrs. Walsh, Cantrill and Daniels were arrested by Lieut. Col. Skinner and a detachment of troops, at Walsh's house. Grenfel and the witness Shanks were arrested at the Richmond House, and Mr. Marmaduke was arrested at the residence of Dr. Edwards, No. 70 Adams street. Judge Morris was arrested by Mr. Keefe and members of the police. These arrests were made on the 6th of November. They were arrested upon information which led me to believe that there was on foot a conspiracy to release the prisoners, and get up a revolution in Indiana and Illinois. I regarded the emergency as immediate, and therefore acted promptly. I dared not trust the telegraph and the railroad, for I understood that the Sons of Liberty had men employed upon them. There were one hundred and fifty men arrested in all. They were principally from the South and Central Illinois, and had lately arrived in Chicago. These were mainly from Fayette and Christian counties, Illinois. These were arrested in grog-shops, boarding-houses, under the pavements, and in every part of the city All of these men were arrested from their appearance and description, and by their looks were taken to be vagabonds. There were but few of them armed. They asserted that they came to Chicago to see the city. Some of them stated that they belonged to the Sons of Liberty, and some from the Southern army; about one tenth came from the Southern army. These bushwhackers were arrested partly by the city police, partly by citizens, and some by soldiers.

Have heard of such an organization as Klingmen's men. Most of them coming from Christain and Fayette counties. It was chiefly made up of deserters from the Federal army and those who ran away from the draft, and was intended to resist the draft and all the operations of the Provost Marshal and the General government in the prosecution of the war. I succeeeded in capturing the Captain and Lieutenant, and the principal men of the organization. It was not an organization under the United States or State law. I received all of these men up to the 8th of November, and all being strangers, I took them in.

I do not know the exact size of Camp Douglas, but believet it compises from 60 to 70 acres of land. The prisoners square proper, covers about 20 acres. In November last it was enclosed by a board fence 12 feet in height and made of lumber an inch and a quarter in thickness. The boards were placed endways and were nailed from the inside. The outside sentinels were stationed on a parapet about three feet from the top of the fence on the outside. The camp was more easily assailable from without and less defensible than if the attack was made from inside.

The Judge Advocate here exhibited to the witness a plan of the camp found on the person of one of the conspirators.

Colonel Sweet.—The map is very roughly drawn and is a little out of proportion in detail, but is a correct drawing of the camp as it was in August and September of last year. The outlines are precisely the same. As shown on the map there were then 40 barracks in the prison square. This number is now increased. The Guard-house and small tents on the west side of the camp are also moved now. The barracks marked "Yankee Barracks" is the correct position of the barracks occupied by the garrison in Garrison Square. The building marked "Douglas House" on the South side of the camp is, I suppose the Douglas University. It is a magnificent building and is located about eighteen or twenty rods from the camp fence, and overlooks the entire camp. One hundred men, or even fifty men, stationed in that building, would command Camp Douglas, and almost make it untenable to any force. During the session of the Democratic Convention, and until the danger was over, I stationed two companies near that building. I had in my charge a prisoner named John T. Shanks at that time; he was there when I assumed the command of the camp, on the second of May, 1864. He was a clerk in the office for the commissary of prisoners. He applied to me to take the oath of allegiance during the summer. His application went through me to the Commissary General of Prisoners with my approval. I never approved these applications unless I was fully convinced that the applicant was desirous of becoming a loyal citizen. The application was not granted, but I made it the basis of communication to Commissary General that Shanks desired to serve the United States, and to take the oath. In this camp there were some men who were more largely entrusted than others. Shanks was a paroled prisoner, having the freedom of Garrison Square during the day time. There were others there in the same condition—a man named Grey, and clerks in the medical department. Shanks was allowed to go to the city two or three times in company with an officer. The prisoners are never permitted to have any funds. I gave Shanks a dollar. Shanks never used a *nomme de plume* that I am aware of. The prisoners were not allowed to have any money, nor did they possess any unless they obtained it secretly. Shanks, however, had, I believe, one dollar, which I gave him. When a prisoner is brought to camp he is thoroughly searched, and any money taken from him is placed in hands of the Prisoner's Accountant, to be drawn, if required, in provisions from the sutler. Letters are all opened, and any money they contain similarly applied. I sent Shanks to the house of Judge Morris on the the 3rd of November, because five men had just escaped from the camp, and I traced them, I believe, to that house. I asked Shanks if he would not like to do the government a service. He replied that he would, when I told him that I wanted him to go to the house of Morris and represent that he had violated his parole and escaped, and if possible must be secreted with the other prisoners. I then sent for Keefe, and the two went to the city in a buggy. I followed on the street cars, and went to my office, No. 90 Washington street, where I had told Shanks to report if he could not find the prisoners. After I had been there a short time, Shanks came to me and gave me $30, which he said Mrs. Morris had given to him, with the exception of one dollar. I do not think he had any money when he went to her house.

I know Maurice Langhorne. He introduced himself to me on the 5th of November, by showing me a letter from Secretary Seward to Secretary Stanton, recommending that he be allowed to take the oath of allegiance. He gave me some information regarding the plot, but I did not know whether or not to take him into my confidence. At a subsequent meeting, the next day, however, at the Tremont House, I determined that he was an honest, reliable man, and one who could be trusted. He has been of great value to me, and his information was ever correct. On the 12th of November, after the first arrests were made, I first offered to employ him. I asked him to identify all who he remembered having seen in Canada, in connection with the conspirators, and arrest them. He personally arrested the witness, John Maughan, at the Tremont House. He gave me information of the ammunition in Walsh's house, and subsequent facts proved that his information was perfectly correct. I gave him the fictitious name of Johnson. He never acted as a detective, but simply aided in arresting men he had known before. Shanks worked for the Government ever since I knew him. Up to the 12th of November, he received no pay, and after that got $100 a month as his salary. I believe, however, that I previously gave him one month's salary, to purchase some citizen's clothing. Of the arms seized at Walsh's house I have the shot guns at camp. The pistols were entrusted to Col. Hough to arm a citizens' patrol, and he has not returned them. I do not know the exact number of arms we captured. There were about 354 revolvers and 200 double barreled guns found in his house, and thirty cavalry carbines in his barn in the city; the latter weapons were not loaded, but those found in his dwelling were. There were also from 14,000 to 15,000 rounds of cartridges, and some roughly made buckshot cartridges, the number of which I do not remember. We also obtained some arms from other persons arrested, I mean the bushwhackers. I do not think that any arms were found on any of the prisoners at the bar, except, possibly, Grenfell.

It will be interesting to the citizens of Chicago, if not in other localities, to peruse the following report from a newspaper, which has perhaps done more than any other in the United States, to aid and promote the interests and cause of the rebels—a paper, the baneful influence of which Gen. Burnside well knew, and would have crushed out; but the editor of that print was suffered to proceed on his dirty and devilish work, and most industrious has he been. The most loathsome reptiles, as we see in the economy of nature, have their uses; "the toad, ugly and venomous, wears yet a precious jewel in his head;" the spider, cunning and fierce, is not without his uses; the wily serpent has his office, the viper was not made in vain, and as the mighty plan of the Great Creator of the Universe is above the comprehension of man, we may wonder at, but never understand why beings in the guise of men, were ever formed, who know no patriotism, no gratitude, none of the nobler attributes of man, and whose mission seems but destruction to his race, and deadly enmity to his country. The *Times*, who in these days of victory and triumph of Union arms, would "steal the livery of heaven to serve the devil in," and prate of its devotion to the Union, furnishes us some information it were well for good citizens to know, and which we will presume is (unlike most statements in that concern) reliable.

LIST OF McCLELLAN ORGANIZATIONS IN THE CITY OF CHICAGO.

We extract the following from the Chicago *Times* of October 20, 1864. It will do to keep for reference. The comments which preface the list are from the pen of the editor of that delectable print. The only comment we need make is, that almost every man whose name is upon the list, was a member of the Chicago Temple of the Sons of Liberty, in good and regular standing with the order:

"There is at present a thoroughly organized and efficient McClellan club in nearly every ward in the city. The good that has resulted to the democratic party from these organizations is more than can be readily imagined. They have done much to stimulate men to an interest in the issues of the day which never would have been felt but for the exertions of the clubs. In those wards where these organizations have not already been formed, meetings are appointed to take place this week for the purpose of forming them, and by the next Sabbath there will be one in every ward in the city. Ordinarily the clubs meet once a week, but they convene oftener for special purposes. There are always speakers ready to address these meetings, being local candidates, speakers residing in the wards where the meetings are held, or speakers from abroad. Below will be found a list of the McClellan clubs now in effect, together with the names of their officers:

FIRST WARD.

President, Chas. W. Patten; Vice-Presd'nt, P. D. Parks; Secretary, J. O. More; Executive Committee, George S. Kimberly, William Y. Daniels, Dr. J. A. Hahn, Augustus Banyon, Andrew Schall.

SECOND WARD.

President, William Baragwanatle; Vice-Presidents, Anton Berg, Dr. E. W. Edwards, Samuel Duncan; Secretary, James Rattray; Treasurer, F. E. Barber; Executive Committee, F. E. Barber, James Rattray, C. C. Strawn, J. Schlossman, P. M. Donelan, H. L. Stewart, F. Cahill, Thos. Tilley, William Hull.

THIRD WARD.

President, Geo. A. Meech; Vice-President, Stephen A. Barrett; Secretary, Benjamin F. Smith; Treasurer, John Dalton; Executive Committee, Joshua L. Marsh, John Schauk, James McGrath.

FOURTH WARD.

President, A. A. Campbell; Vice-President, M. L. Kuth; Treasurer, Thomas Horless; Secretary, L. W. Binz; Executive Committee, I. H. Ferrell, Mark Kimball, Charles Walsh.

FIFTH WARD.

President, Mark Sheridan; First Vice-President, M. C. Quinn; Second Vice-President, Jas. Brennan; Secretary, Christopher Dennis; Assistant Secretary, James Fox; Treasurer, John Reid; Executive Committee, Constantine Kann, John Keyes, John Myers, L. J. Prout, John Lyons, Michael McDermott, Michael Finucan, Thomas Barry.

SEVENTH WARD.

President, E. Gilmore; First Vice-President, D. W. Quirk; Second Vice-President, Gotthard Schaaff; Secretary, M A. Donahue; Treasurer, Joseph Sherwin; Executive Committee, John Comisky, J. K. Boland, P. Caraher, T. Tully, and T. E. Courtney.

NINTH WARD.

President, S. S. Elson; Vice-President, R. O'Malley; Secretary, A. S. Morrison; Treasurer, P. Moran; Executive Committee, E. F. Runnison, P. S. Hade, Michael Gerrity.

TENTH WARD.

President, Hiram M. Chase; Vice-President, H. N. Hahn; Secretary, A. L. Amberg; Treasurer, T. T. Gurney; Executive Committee, D. W. Manchester, M. McCurdy, Joseph Hogan.

FOURTEENTH WARD.

President, Joseph Kuhn; Vice-President, P. Stech; Treasurer, John Schierer; Secretary, J. B. Winkelman; Executive Committee, B. Docter, Fred. Licht, N. Gerten.

The *Times* adds:

"The above list gives all the names that have ever been published. In some of the wards there are two clubs, and yet the permanent organization of either has never been given. In some other wards they have no permanent organization, but elect officers at each weekly meeting. In the other wards clubs will be formed within a few days. It should be borne in mind that the above clubs are independent of the Invincible Club, which is not a mere ward organization, but represents the whole city."

CHAP. XVII.

PLOT TO ASSASSINATE THE PRESIDENT OF THE UNITED STATES—THE CONSUMATION OF THE INFERNAL PLOT—DEATH OF PRESIDENT LINCOLN AND DEADLY ASSAULT UPON SECRETARY SEWARD—RESOLUTIONS OF THE CHICAGO BOARD OF TRADE.

During the autumn of 1864, at a meeting of the Sons of Liberty, in Chicago, a proposition was introduced which contemplated the raising of a fund of fifty thousand dollars, which was to be expended in payment of the services of some person who would undertake to assassinate the President of the United States. This was an informal proceeding, the meeting having just adjourned, but it was discussed by several of the leading members, who declared that the "extermination of tyrants was obedience to God."

What say you, citizens of Chicago, concerning the band of traitors in your midst, who meditate and discuss such crimes as make the soul sicken, and the face blanch with horror; would not any honest man deliver this department of Jeff Davis' most efficient allies into the hands of the United States Government, by any means Heaven might place in his power? If there is a man so fastidious of propriety, so mindful of selfish considerations, that he would not, then, in our opinion, that man is a coward, a traitor, an imbecile too weak to punish, and deserving the scorn and contumely of his countrymen, for all coming time. This proposition was the next day reported in a dispatch to Col. Sweet, and is now on file in his office. It may be that the persons who discussed the proposition, would not themselves have undertaken the accomplishment of the deed, but the *animus* of the party was thus rendered apparent, and the proposition was gravely considered and discussed. This occurred soon after an interview, by the writer, with Maj. Gen. Hooker, at the Tremont House, in Chicago, in October. It had been often said that in case Lincoln was elected, he should never be inaugurated, implying that his life would be terminated before that event. Some of the very parties who made these threats, have since been prisoners in Camp Douglas, but are now at large. On the night of the 14th of April, 1865, assassins, who were, doubtless, members of the Sons of Liberty, in accordance with the same spirit in which that Order came into existence, and was conducted from first to last, consumated their hellish designs by shooting President Lincoln, and stabbing Secretary Seward. The nation now mourns the loss of the noble martyr of freedom, the truest heart, the most devoted patriot, the sincere advocate of republican institutions, and the friend of the people. In every city, town, and village, and hamlet of the land, is sincere mourning; deepest grief swells the hearts and dim the eyes of all who have hearts to feel, and fountains of tears, for the greatest bereavement that has ever befallen our nation. The emblems of mourning, the solemn tolling of bells, the universal gloom which overshadows our land, all impress upon our hearts the terrible affliction that has come upon us, and while we would bow reverently before Him who doeth all things well, and whose wise purpose in this chastening of our already sorrowing people may not now be apparent, we cannot repress the just indignation of our souls that moves us to the enactment of that stern justice which is uncompromising, and which cries to Heaven for vengeance, which nerves our hearts and hands to deeds, the generous, noble, President of the nation, now silent in the tomb, would have softened or averted. Villians have slain the man whose heart was large enough to take into his affections and paternal love, the whole country,—the man who knew no North, no South, no East, no West, but whose devotion to the best good of the people, was the ruling motive of a life so full of honors and usefulness. The North had no friend like Lincoln! The South had no friend like Lincoln! And, as our noble armies now march onward to victory, and crush out beneath their iron heel, the last vestige of treason, the memory of Lincoln will prove a watch-word of magic power; soldiers will remember the entreaties, the offers of pardon, the paternal affection of the noble Lincoln, and the base ingratitude of the demon who consigned him to the tomb; they who have commended his magnanimity, his humanity, his hopefulness, his reluctance to deal out stern justice, which required hard blows—such of our fellow-citizens will now, with holy indignation, rise in their might, and sweep from the land those whose treason is heard, and whose bloody hand is uplifted, aye, and those who devise their hellish schemes in secret chambers and hiding places in our own cities and towns. "Remember Lincoln," will be the battle-cry of our boys as they encounter armed treason in the field, and "Remember Lincoln," should be the watchword of friends of freedom at home, when hesitating in clemency, to strike down Copperheads who seek to embarrass the government, and hope for, prophicy and delight in its reverses upon the field of contest. Remember Lincoln and Seward ye men who would now compromise by any and all sacrifices, with a people who have sought to destroy our country, and have stricken down the pride of our nation, the noblest of our land, and the champion of liberty. The Chicago Board of Trade assembled upon the morning of the 15th of April, and adopted the following resolutions:

Resolved, That this Board has heard with mingled sentiments of grief and horror of the foul assassination, by accursed traitors, of Abraham Lincoln, President of the United States.

Resolved, That we mourn in the deepest sorrow his loss as a national calamity. His persevering and devoted patriotism through the dark days of the Republic: his wisdom alike in the hour of trial and triumph, have embalmed his memory in the hearts of his countrymen, and encircled his fame with a glory which time can never tarnish.

Resolved, That in this infernal act we see but another instance of the demoniac hate of the slave power, arrested by the strong arm of the government, under the heaven inspired leadership of Abraham Lincoln, in its career of treason, murder and despotism; and we are admonish d anew to insist upon no compromise with the infamy, and upon the condign punishment by the mailed hand of power, and the strong arm of the law, of treason and its abettors, wherever found.

Resolved, That in our capacity of business men and citizens, we vow eternal hate to the treachery and treason of the rebellion, which, in addition to its before unnumbered crimes, has added the cowardly assassination of Abraham Lincoln in the vain hope of destroying this Republic.

Resolved, Th t in deep humiliation, we bow before the God of battles and of Nations, and, in this hour of our grand triumph and overwhelming sorrow, we reverently consign to His all-guiding wisdom the destiny of this Republic, and pray Him still to have it in His holy keeping.

Resolved, That the members of this Board, who have, from the war's beginning, felt it their duty, as it has been their privilege and their pride, to stand by the nation and its President and all its constituted leaders, loyally aiding and encouraging, as they could, the Cabinet and the Army in the gigantic struggle of the past four years, do now solemnly, unitedly, in the presence f Almighty God, and in humble reliance on the Divine help, pledge our full, unreserved, and trusting support to the Government of these United States, and to the men who now constitutionally succeed to the authority and powers, now laid down by the great and good man, who has fallen a precious and holy sacrifice on the altar of his country. And the members of this Board, in making this solemn pledge, do the same, not for themselves only, but in behalf of the loyal and patriotic people of the Northwest, who have freely offered their first-born, and best beloved for their coun ry's existence, security and honor.

Resolved, That the members of this Board express their profound and respectful sympathy with the bereaved family of the deceased, and with the associates of the departed in the Cabinet, as well as all the members of the national councils, in the tragic and deplorable events in which they share so largely.

CHAP. XVIII.

HYPOCRICY OF COPPERHEAD NEWSPAPERS—COMPLICITY WITH ASSASSI-NATION—THE LEADERS AND THEIR VICTIMS.

During the month of February, by Executive clemency, a number of Copperheads were released from confinement in Washington, where they had been placed as a measure of public safety. The *Times* published, and other Copperhead papers echoed the following. That paper now, in a very pious spirit, piteously urges, and the prints of like character also echo it, that "there should be no more party strife," "no more rancor," that it has not stabbed the President since he was shot, and the office is now draped with deep mourning. Aminadab Sleek is going to them as a comforter, and as tears mitigate woe, he bears with him an onion. The *Times* says:

"We submit that this fact should damn this Administration, not only for all time, but, if there be justice hereafter, to all eternity. There is not a single civilized government in existence to-day, against which can be charged a similar display of tyranny. With the title of being the freest government of modern ages, we have shewn ourselves to be one whose disregard of right and whose outrageous assumptions of power are only paralleled in the reign of despots.

T e liberty of fifty men may seem a small affair; but the matter has not so much reference to the magnitude of the offence as it has to the principle which underlies it. The moment Mr. Lincoln, or Mr. Seward, or any other man. dares to deprive one per on of his liberty without due process of law, that moment has the government been changed from one of the people to an autocracy—a tyranny. If any man to day is free in this country, it is not because he is a good citizen, surrounded by the protection of the laws, but simply because Seward or Lincoln has not chosen to order his incarceration.

The epitaph of posterity upon this people is easily anticipated. It will be—died 24,000,-000 of whites, who lost their liberties and lives in an attempt to give a fictitious freedom to 4,000,000 negroes."

"*Sic semper tyrannis!*" exclaims Booth, who has read the above article, and the mission of the *Times* is accomplished, and it now wants "no more party rancor."

"Out of my sight thou serpent! That name best
Befits thee with him leagu'd, thyself as false!"

The palpable hypocricy of rebel sympathizers, can now only excite contempt. Who that read the evidence of Clement L. Vallandigham, before the military commission in Cincinnati, gave him credit for sincerity when he said substantially had he supposed there was a plot against the Government, he would have been the first to oppose or expose it. Have the people forgotten Mr. Vallandigham's record? Have his Dayton neighbors forgotten his cry of "Ocoon," the cry of distress of the Order to which he belonged, and which was to summon Sons of

Liberty to his rescue, when arrested by the Government? Have they forgotten Vallandigham's visit to Fulton county, Illinois, during the autumn of 1864, and its consequences? This county was the stamping ground of the leaders of the treasonable organization, which has been dissected, and whose head and heart are now in a state of decomposition. In that county Assistant Provost Marshal Phelps was shot, there too enrolling officer Criss was shot; in that county is Lewiston, where resides S. Corning Judd, Esq., the Grand Commander of the Sons of Liberty in the State of Illinois. C. L. Vallandigham was the Supreme Commander of the Order in the United States. This Order inaugurated the new warfare at the instance of the Southern rebel leaders—inaugurated assassination. This order began with Provost Marshals and enrolling officers, and ended—if indeed the loyal people *will* it to have ended—with the assassination of the best, the wisest, the most deeply loved President since the immortal Washington. It is the education of Copperhead prints, and Copperhead secret societies that has fitted the instruments of death, and our indulgence which has fostered them.

Vallandigham's party had been defeated, his greatness had departed, and to wheel into line and "keep step to the music of the Union," was not for him, and as Milton's creation once exclaimed, so might he have uttered:

>"And in my choice
>To reign is worth ambition, though in hell;
>Better to reign in hell than serve in heaven.
>But wherefore let me then our faithful friends,
>The associates and co-partners of our loss,
>Lie thus astonished on the oblivion pool,
>And call them not to share with us their part
>In this unhappy mansion; or once more
>With rallied arms to try what may be yet
>Regained in heaven, or what more lost in hell."

And so Clement L. Vallandigham became Supreme Commander of the Sons of Liberty.

Who is S. Corning Judd, who testifies before the Commission that "*the organization* (Sons of Liberty) *was being used in Indiana and Missouri for improper purposes*"? Who is he that says the organization in Chicago "was looked upon by many of the leaders with great distrust; many of those connected with the order in Chicago were radical, extreme men, and understood to be men of little standing or character"? that one of the delegates from Missouri stated his belief that the order in that State was in favor of "giving aid and comfort to the Confederates"? When Judd made these statements upon the stand, all loyal papers, with one accord, declared that the evidence fully warranted the arrests, in the manner and at the time they were made. No fair-minded man *then* could come to any other conclusion. Who, we ask, is S. Corning Judd? Stump-speakers, last fall, would have said that he was the "Democratic" candidate for Lieutenant Governor—and so he was. The Gubernatorial ticket bore the name of James C. Robinson for Governor, and S. Corning Judd for Lieutenant Governor—the former a man who, in Congress, voted against "fighting, crushing, and destroying" the rebellion. Both Robinson and Judd were Sons of Liberty, and to them Copperheads fondly turned, and had they carried the State, anarchy and bloodshed would have been the consequence; and, indeed, in the expressed opinion of Judge Morris, " had they carried the State, he cared not who might be President, for they would possess the reins of the General Government." S. Corning Judd sought to serve his own ends by controlling the Sons of Liberty, and failing in this, he gave the cold-shoulder to his Brig.-General (Walsh), when, in consequence of executing the edicts of the order, he found himself a close prisoner for the horrid doctrine of secession; *he* must be tried and convicted, but the Grand Commander, S. Corning Judd, and the Supreme Commander, C. L. Vallandigham, and the Past Grand Commander, or Major-General, Amos Green, each, severally appear upon the stand against him, and they permitted to go scott free. O, cursed doctrine of secession!

> "S. stretch'd out huge in length the arch-fiend lay,
> Chain'd on the burning lake; nor ever thence
> Had risen or heaved his head, but that the will
> And high permission of All-ruling Heaven
> Left him at large to his own dark designs;
> That with reiterated crimes he might
> Heap on himself damnation, while he sought
> Evil to others."

If Vallandigham, if Judd, if Green, if Barrett, and if the many equally guilty persons released from custody go unpunished, then "Justice, thou art fled to brutish beasts, and men have lost their reason." Not that we would contradict Judd in the least in aught that he has said against the Chicago temple, but we would tell him that we *know* the Chicago temple, so far from taking the lead in radicalism, was behind the order in Peoria, in Bloomington, in Dubuque, in St. Louis, Louisville, and many other places. Give the devil his due. In some places the boldness of Copperheadism induced prominent members of the Sons of Liberty to approach members of Congress, with their base proposals to enter the order.

CHAP. XIX.

EXTINCTION OF SLAVERY—NO CONCILIATION WITH TRAITORS—DOWN WITH COPPERHEADS AT HOME.

In a publication of this character, it will not be expected we should review either the causes which led to the great rebellion, with its hydra heads and its sad consequences; but in closing, and especially in view of the terrible tragedy which has plunged a nation in deepest grief, we cannot refrain from saying, that the last most diabolical deed was not the act of individual madness, of personal hate and passion, it was the culmination of the hatred by the slave power of the principle of liberty, and the champion of freedom. It was not because the assassin felt in his heart a hatred of Abraham Lincoln, but because he, and the people at whose instigation he acted, hated the apostle of liberty, and the instrument in the hand of God for the accomplishment of a great and mighty work. Although it was the purpose of this band of murderers to assassinate the President and the whole Cabinet, it was not from personal malice against them as men, but the enemy sought by the destruction of the exponents of a free government, to give new life to the expiring representation of the slave power. So antagonistic was freedom to slavery that it was impossible to permanently embody the representatives of these principles with a republican government, which should be perfect in its formation, wise and just in its action, the hope of the liberty loving people throughout the world, and the pride and glory of American citizens. Every year since the adoption of the old Constitution, have discordant elements cropped out, and incidents transpired, which demonstrated to every rational mind, that as time rolled on, the accumulation of combustible elements would ultimately explode, and shake the civilized world to its center.

The facts that Northern teachers, Northern clergymen, Northern mercantile agents, Northern men upon business or pleasure, travelling at the South, and unwilling to stultify themselves, or become passive approvers and admirers of the "peculiar institution," were treated with all possible indignities, and might count themselves fortunate if they escaped with their lives. So complete was the universal devotion to slavery in all sections of the South, and so baneful its effects upon the people, that all other considerations were made subservient to this. For slavery, friends were alienated, hatred established, so bitter in its extent that only death could appease it. It demoralized the entire people; it found its way with all its horrid moral deformities, into the very capitol; it caused the muderous assault of Brooks upon Charles Sumner in the Senate, and the many altercations and bitter harangues which have from time to time disgraced our National Congress; it was its cropping out that caused the fearless and noble President Andy Johnson, to threaten to hang Jeff. Davis—and which he may yet be called upon to perform ;—it was slavery that devised the doctrine of secession; that has led to the deadly conflict upon hundreds of battle fields, and has spilled the best blood of our nation, and caused mourning and gloom all over the face of our once happy land. What wonder then, that the noble Lincoln, who, in the sincerity of his heart, and in the dictates of superior wisdom, who, seeing and appreciating the encroachments and horrors of slavery, not only to the people in bondage, but to the citizens of our country in every section—who wonders that Lincoln, whose name is immortal, especially for his extirpation of this curse, should be singled out by the demon of slavery, and assigned by Davis, his prophet, for a violent death. Thank God, the cancer is extirpated so thoroughly, that its fibres of death can never again form to threaten destruction to our land. True, the operation has been most painful, and no anesthetic agent has been employed; the suffering has been fearful, and the country has, to its extremities, trembled with anguish; but it is over now.

The assassination of the President was the will of Jeff. Davis, whispered in the temples of the Sons of Liberty or American Knights, into the ears of those of the members of the Orders, who had made the most proficiency in their teachings, and these beings, true to their oaths, went forth upon their mission of blood.

The following " gems," from the debates in the Democratic National Convention, will be read with interest now and in future time:

S. S. Cox, said:

" He had attempted in his own city, a few weeks since, to show, in a very quiet way, that ABRAHAM LINCOLN HAD DELUGED THE COUNTRY WITH BLOOD, created a debt of four thousand million of dollars, sacrificed two millions of human lives, and filled the land with grief and mourning."

A pious man, who had listened attentively to his remarks, sang out "G—d d—n him."

" For less offenses than Mr. Lincoln had been guilty of, the English people had chopped off the head of the first Charles. IN HIS OPINION, LINCOLN AND DAVIS OUGHT TO BE BROUGHT TO THE SAME BLOCK TOGETHER."

C. Chauncey Burr, editor of several Copperhead New York journals, said :

"And it was a wonder that they had a Cabinet and men who carried out the infamous orders of the gorilla tyrant that usurped the Presidential chair."

Capt. Koontz, of Pittsburg, an ardent McClellan leader, said :

" If Democrats catch Lincoln's bloody spies among them, they must cut their d—d throats, that's all. [Applause.] It is the duty of every American to vote for a peace candidate."

Baker, of Michigan, said :

" Let us hurl that usurper from power. Never till that day comes when the usurper and his victim meet at the judgment seat, can he be punished for his wrongs, for his conspiracy against American liberty."

Benjamin Allen, of New York, said :

" The people will soon rise, AND IF THEY CANNOT PUT LINCOLN OUT OF POWER BY THE BALLOT THEY WILL BY THE BULLET." [Loud cheers.]

Mr. Stambaugh, a delegate from Ohio, said:

"That, if he was called upon to elect between the freedom of the nigger and disunion and separation, he should choose the latter." (Cheers.)

"They might search hell over and they could not find a worse President than Abraham Lincoln."

Hon. Mr. Trainor, of Ohio, said:

"He would urge the people to be freemen, and HURL ABRAHAM LINCOLN AND HIS MINIONS FROM POWER."

Henry Clay Dean, said:

"In the presence of the face of Camp Douglas and all the satraps of Lincoln, that the American people were ruled by felons. Lincoln had never turned a dishonest man out of office, or kept an honest man in. [A voice—'What have you to say of Jeff. Davis?'] I have nothing to say about him. LINCOLN IS ENGAGED IN A CONTROVERSY WITH HIM, AND I NEVER INTERFERE BETWEEN BLACK DOGS."

"He blushed that such a felon should occupy the highest place in the gift of the people. PERJURY AND LARCENY WERE WRITTEN OVER HIM AS OFTEN AS WAS 'ONE DOLLAR' ON THE ONE DOLLAR BILLS OF THE BANK OF THE STATE OF INDIANA. (Cries of the 'old villian.') The Democracy were for peace."

W. W. O'Brien, of Peoria, also threatened "to try him as Charles the first was tried, as a tyrant and a traitor, and if they found him guilty to hang him.

The essential unity of Copperheadism with assassination, appears in the following remarks of Koontz, of Pennsylvania:

"Shall more wives be made widows, and more children fatherless, and greater hate be stirred up between children of the same glorious constitution? IF NOT WE MUST PUT OUR FOOT UPON THE TYRANT'S NECK, and destroy it, The Democratic government must be raised to power, and Lincoln with his Cabinet of rogues, thieves and spies, be driven to destruction. What shall we do with him?]A voice—"Send him here, and I'll make a coffin for him, d—n him."]

As we review the events which have transpired during this war, we are strikingly impressed with the magnanimity, the forbearance, the humanity of the loyal States in their relations to the rebels in arms, and we are also impressed with the great lack of the exhibition of these qualities—the most enobling in national character—on the part of the so-called Southern Confederacy. From the hour of firing upon Fort Sumter to the present moment, the war has not been waged by the rebels as if in defense of the great principles of truth and justice, but with the malignity, the cruelty and barbarity which would, in many instances, put to blush the savages upon our western borders. In our dealing with them, the honor, integrity, fidelity and dignity of the nation have never been forgotten; and the policy of the noble President, laid low by the hand of the assassin, was never to give blows when words would answer,—never to exact by force what might be attained by reasoning,—and never, under any circumstances, to forget those qualities which make a nation truly great, the first and chief of which is charity. How has our enemy failed to appreciate this? The manner in which the warfare has been waged by the South will be mentioned by historians as cruel, dishonorable and disgraceful to people of a Christian nation. Failing of success upon the field, we find the Davis Government countenancing guerrilla warfare, burning bridges, murdering unarmed citizens, and desolating the homes of unoffending people, and committing piracy upon the high seas. Still failing of success and losing ground daily, but driven to desperation by the apparent hopelessness of their cause, they sink to the depth of infamy by establishing among us secret orders, the aim of which is to educate men of base passions to deeds of dark dishonor and unmeasured infamy; men who receiving such instruction will concoct schemes for the burning of cities, for the liberation of their prisoners; and, lastly, they have sunk so low in the mire of dishonor, impelled by savage ferocity and hate, that it would appear folly, if not downright criminality to longer deal with them on the principles of liberality and gentleness, which has marked our conduct hitherto. It was our generosity, our mildness, our spirit of conciliation that moved the hand of the demon who slew the country's truest friend. Let it be so no longer! Let rebels feel that we are terribly in earnest. Let heavy blows be struck, and struck without delay, and let there be no exhibition of concession or conciliation, till the enemy sue for peace upon the terms the country proclaims. As well make Copperheads Christians or honest men, as to attempt by gentleness longer to subdue rebels, whose weapons are firebrands and assassins' daggers. It is futile; try it no longer. Said the great French advocate of justice, when he was charged with being sanguinary, because he so frequently punished murder with death, "You tell me that it is bloody work, and sinful in the sight of Heaven to execute men; so it is, and I am disposed to desist, and I will, the moment men stop the crime of murder." So will we show clemency, when our enemy has laid down his arms, and not before.

Another measure by our people would be attended with salutary results—the extermination of Copperheadism at home. Who helped to form secret societies of Sons of Liberty and kindred organizations, so industriously and so efficiently as editors of Copperhead publications. It is in these orders that assassins are trained, and prepared for their fiendish mission. Henceforth let the people—the loyal people of the most glorious country on which the sun shines—swear by the memory of our much loved and deeply lamented President, that henceforth no paper shall print, no man shall utter sentiments of treason, under the penalty of incurring that summary punishment, the righteous indignation of a sorrowing, long suffering people may inflict. If the people resolve to endure the curse of home treason no longer, and let Copperheads know that they can no longer co-operate with Jeff. Davis in any part of our land, we shall never again be called upon to aid in suppressing or exposing a North-Western Conspiracy, or any plot against our country, in any section of our land.

CHAP. XX.

TRIAL OF THE CHICAGO CONSPIRATORS—THE WITNESSES AND THE TESTIMONY.

When our troops entered Richmond, among other rebel documents found was a bill, offered in secret session of the rebel House of Representatives, January 30th, 1865, establishing a Secret Service Bureau, for the employment of secret agents, "either in the Confederate States, or within the enemy's lines, or in any foreign country," and authorizing the chief officer "to organize such a system *for the application of new means of warfare approved*, and of secret service agencies, as may tend best to secure the objects of the establishment of the bureau."

The trial, conviction, sentence, and execution of Capt. Beall, for piracy on the lakes, and of Kennedy, for incendiarism in New York, are still fresh in the recollection of our readers. That these men were acting under instructions from the bureau of secret service of Jeff. Davis, no rational person can doubt. These acts were but incidents in the grand conspiracy at the North; the guilty parties, who suffered death, were but the instruments of others, and the members of the secret organizations, who were cognizant of these acts and purposes, though yet unwhipped of justice, are more guilty, in the sight of Heaven, than the wretches who undertook the execution of the hellish design, and for which they suffered ignominious death.

After the discovery of the purposes and acts of the leaders of the Sons of Liberty in Illinois, in co-operation with rebels, and the arrests detailed in a former chapter, a Military Commission was convened in Cincinnati for the trial of the prisoners, Morris, Walsh, Grenfell, Anderson, Daniels, Cantril, Marmaduke and Semmes, upon a charge of conspiring to sack and burn Chicago, and to liberate the prisoners in Camp Douglas.

The Commission consisted of the following named officers:

C. D. Murray, Colonel 89th Indiana Volunteers, President Commission.
Ben. Spooner, Colonel 83d Indiana Volunteers.
N. C. Macræ, Major United States Army.
P. Vous Radowitz, Lieutenant-Colonel United States Army.
S. P. Lee, Major 6th Regiment Veteran Reserve Corps.
M. N. Wiswell, Colonel Veteran Reserve Corps.
R. P. DeHart, Colonel 128th Indiana Volunteers.
S. H. Lathrop, Lieuteant-Colonel, A. 1. G.
Albert Heath, Lieutenant-Colonel 100th Regiment Indiana Volunteers.

CONFESSION OF MRS. MORRIS, B. S., AND HER SENTENCE.

CINCINNATI, Feb. 13.

The following is Mrs. Morris' confession:

McLEAN BARRACKS, CINCINNATI, Feb. 5, 1865.

To Maj.-Gen. J. Hooker, Commanding Northern Department, Cincinnati, O.:

General—I was arrested in Chicago, on the 11th day of December, by the United States authorities, charged with assisting rebel prisoners to escape, and relieving them with money and clothing; also, with holding correspondence with the enemy. I desire to state the facts of the case, to confess the truth, and to ask such clemency at your hands as may be consistent with your duty as an officer of the government. I was born and reared in Kentucky. My home was in the South till within the last ten years, my connections and friends all being there. I had sympathy with them, though I was as much opposed to the secession movement as any one could be. Having a large acquaintance in Kentucky, I was charged with the distribution of a great deal of clothing and money among the prisoners in Camp Douglas, Chicago, sent to them by their friends, and which was done under the supervision of the proper officers of the camp. This I continued to do up to the time of my arrest, and in this way I made the acquaintance, and was understood to be the friend of the prisoners in camp.

In the early part of last winter, an escaped prisoner named John Harrington, came to me and asked for assistance. He stated that he was going to Canada for the purpose of completing his education. I gave him money to the amount I believe of $20. Some time in the summer of the past year, a rebel prisoner named Charles Swager, a young man who had escaped from the cars while being conveyed to Rock Island, came to me for assistance. I gave him a coat, a pair of boots, and some money, to the amount I believe, of $15. There were two or three others that I had reason to believe were escaped prisoners, whose names I do not know. These I assisted with money, and to one of them I gave some clothing. There were some others to whom I gave money and clothing, that I did not at the time know were rebel prisoners, but who afterwards I had reason to believe were such.

I received letters from Capt. J. B, Castleman of the rebel army, and sent him verbal messages in return. He called at my house, and remained for a little while. Capt. Hines, also of the Confederate army, called and ate at my house once during last summer.

I beg to be released from my present imprisonment, and promise that, if my prayer is granted, I will henceforth conduct myself as a truly loyal woman, without in any way interfering with the government or aiding its enemies.

Witness my hand and seal, this 5th day of Februrary, 1865.   MARY B. MORRIS.

The following is Gen. Hooker's order relative to Mrs. Morris:

HEADQUARTERS NORTHERN DEPARTMENT, }
CINCINNATI, O., Feb. 10, 1865. }

[*Extract.*]

Mrs. Mary B. Morris, now in confinement at McLean barracks, in the city of Cincinnati, O., charged with giving aid and comfort to the enemy, assisting rebel prisoners to escape, and other disloyal practices, will, on or before Monday the 13th inst., be sent south of our military lines, under guard, into the so-called Southern Confederacy. Her sympathy with those in rebellion can there find its natural expression, and a more appropriate theatre of action. It is but just to our government and laws, that the shield of its power should not be thrown over those who are inimical to it, and are giving active aid and sympathy to its enemies. The claim to protection by the government implies the reciprocity of fealty.

Mrs. Mary B. Morris, who was ordered sent out of our lines by paragraph 1 of this order, in consideration of her professions and promises, is permitted to remain on the premises of her father, Edward M. Blackburne, at Spring Station, Woodford county, Ky., on consideration that she complies with the promises accompanying her confession, filed at these headquarters, Feb. 5th, 1865. If such promises are not complied with, the first paragraph of the order to be in full force.

By command of Maj.-Gen. HOOKER.

(Signed) C. H. POTTER,
Assistant Adjutant-General.

The trial of the prisoner Cantril was deferred, owing to serious illness. During the progress of the trial, Anderson committed suicide, and Daniels escaped. [It will be remembered that H. H. Dodd, convicted of treason in Indianapolis, some months ago, and sentenced to suffer the death penalty, also escaped. Neither Daniels or Dodd have been recaptured.] The evidence before the Military Commission elicited most of the important facts embraced in this narrative, and therefore need not be reviewed.

In regard to several of the witnesses before the Military Commission, a few remarks may not be uninteresting. It has been observed by the reader who has carefully perused the foregoing statement, that there were two distinct elements which made up the great conspiracy, viz: The Copperheads, or Sons of Liberty, and Knights of the Golden Circle, and the rebel emissaries both in the Northern States and in Canada. The discovery of the designs, purposes and intents of the former, was made by the writer of this work, who was aided by Robert Alexander. With such aid as we were able to control, we obtained and imparted the information which resulted in the total defeat of the devilish intent of our secret enemies— the Copperheads; the purposes, movements, ends and aims of the *Rebels in Canada*, were reported by Maurice Laughorn, aid by two others. The parties in charge of observing and defeating the two distinct elements, were utter strangers, and had never met or had any communication whatever.

In regard to the writer, it need only be said, that when it was announced to Hon. I. N. Arnold, M. C., Governor Yates, and Brig.-Gen. Paine, that there was a formidable conspiracy against the General Government, embracing many thousand persons in its league, and that its purpose was the subversion of our Government in aid of the rebellion, that their plots were rapidly maturing, and the most alarming consequences might be apprehended, if timely precautions were not observed, all of these gentlemen gave to the matter their earnest and careful attention. It was not the purpose of the writer to proceed with further investigations, except by advice and direction, as it was a work for which he felt wholly unqualified, from his tastes, disposition, professional, and social position, but the arguments of Gen. Paine, which, at this time and place, it is unnecessary to state, but which it is believed neither party will soon forget, decided the matter, and the task was undertaken, and with what success it was attended, let the history of the proceedings in Cincinnati determine. For more than six months, the work was prosecuted with unceasing vigilance, regardless of all other considerations, and although, when he was called to the witness stand, he could not shield himself from the malignant abuse of counsel, by stating *that he had been acting under a commission received from his Government*, yet he then felt morally certain, and that confidence *yet remains unshaken*, that when his true relations to the Government and country, are finally known, his motives, his acts, and his services, will be duly appreciated. He has not been mistaken. The contemptible falsehood of the party who stated that the writer's services had been compensated, or that a claim for compensation had been made, is hereby hurled back into his teeth. Not a dollar, not a dime, has been received, not even for *actual expenses incurred*, and *no claim* whatever has been made—no consideration whatever has been proffered. The service was the result of a deep conviction of duty, a feeling that no citizen should withhold personal sacrifice, even of life and reputation, if the interest of his country demands it. We knew the condition upon which we stepped aside from the agreeable and peaceful avocations of life, and entered upon the task so distasteful, so repulsive, and for a time so thankless. We had reason to know that the shafts of fiendish calumny would assail, that friendship would be broken, *that envy and jealousy would ply their inuendos*, that the Copperhead elements of a fraternity, claiming one of the offenders in its ranks, would assail with bitterness and awaken poignant grief, but no regret, that we should have the hatred of Copperheads, as long as that genus (thank Heaven, short-lived), existed in our land, and be regarded with distrust by those negative persons, who would be for the Union, had they any independence of character; we knew all this would follow, if the assassin's bullet or dagger did not execute the sworn purpose of the Order, but with an abiding faith in the justice of Heaven, with an approving conscience, and our earnest heartfelt prayer for our loved country in her dark hours, we took our course, and our only regret is, that we had not sooner entered upon the work, and thereby frustrated plans which have contributed to our national suffering; for who shall say how many have been its victims, how many homes has it made desolate, how many hearts has it broken, and how many graves now enclose misguided men, and misguided youths, who, educated in its fallacies, lured by its snake-like influence, arrayed themselves against their country, and fell victims to their fanaticism!

We have heard the cry of our Union soldiers at the front, to protect the helpless in the rear, and we have tried to comply. We have given our own near and dear kindred to the bullet and the sword, a sacrifice to freedom, and staunched the life-blood of a dearly loved brother, upon the field of Antietam, and as we wiped away the dew of death, gathering upon his brow, we pledged our life—our all—to the cause of the Union; and if better service might be rendered in vanquishing the secret foe at home, than meeting the more honorable enemy upon the field of battle, we were ready for the work. Had it not been for the potent influence of Copperheads at the North, the counsel, the sympathy, the comfort extended to the rebels, the rebellion would have been put down long ago. Entertaining such views, we shall, under any and all circumstances, and at all times, be a bitter opponent of Copperheadism wherever found, and regard it as legitimate warfare to arrest the assassin of our country, wherever and whenever we can. If the disaffected find comfort in this, let them make the most of it.

ROBERT ALEXANDER.—This gentleman, who is well known to the citizens of Chicago, has held several positions of responsibility and trust, and has ever been a consistent, earnest, devoted advocate of the Union. So intensely Republican in sentiment is he, that the attempt to introduce him into the Sons of Liberty, called forth such opposition that it was thought we should fail in the attempt, and he finally, was only admitted, after he and his sponsor (the writer) had been told, in plain words, accompanied with an oath, that if he proved false to them, *both should die*. For months he bore the opprobrium of a Copperhead, and suffered extreme annoyances in sustaining the role it was his duty to assume. Conscientious, earnest, persevering, patient, with keen perception, and a remarkable power of reading human character, with the experience of an excellent police officer, Mr. Alexander brought to his post of duty high qualifications, and was a valuable, ready and willing assistant. It should be remarked that Mr. Alexander had been informed in May, 1864, that he had been appointed First-Lieutenant in the 53d U. S. Infantry, and supposed he was in the service of the U. S. Government at the time of joining this great undertaking, but the information, though coming from a high source, proved incorrect, and this is one additional reason why the writer made choice of Mr. Alexander. While we know that loyal men will appreciate Mr. Alexander's valuable services, we have yet to learn that he has, thus far, experienced any other satisfaction than the approval of his own heart, and the sincere gratitude of the writer, for his hazardous undertaking, and the able manner in which he performed his duty.

MAURICE LANGHORN, one of the principal government witnesses, was born in Pittsburgh, Penn., and reared in Marysville, Ky. He is a lawyer, and a man of ability. Like many other Kentuckians who were in the South at the time the rebellion broke out, Mr. Langhorn committed himself to the doctrine of secession. In 1861 he enlisted as a private in a Louisiana regiment of heavy artillery. He was subsequently recommended for Colonelcy in the rebel army, but failed to get the appointment. In 1861 he went to Bowling Green, Ky., where he enlisted as a private in the 9th Kentucky Infantry, Col. Thomas H. Hunt, of Louisville, and was transferred to the artillery. He mounted the guns on the fortifications around Bowling Green, and seems to have given great satisfaction. He ran as candidate for representative to the rebel congress from Kentucky, but before the result of the canvass was known, was captured and held eight months as a prisoner of war. Mr. Langhorn subsequently took the oath of allegiance to the United States, and was of great service in reporting the movements and designs of the rebel emissaries in Canada to Col. Sweet. The information Mr. Langhorn gave of those men was reliable, and upon it certain arrests were made. Mr. Langhorn is now a loyal citizen, in its broadest and best sense. Mr. Langhorn is a young man not over twenty-five years of age, of quick, nervous temperament, kind and generous impulses, a man of strong feelings, warm friendship, bitter animosities, and whatever he undertakes, he executes with a will. Of Mr. Langhorn it may be truly said, that while he was a rebel, he was an earnest, active foe, but a true soldier, having a high regard for honor and integrity, loving the State in which he was reared, and ever jealous of her honor and fair name. Mr. Langhorn was a rebel from principle—because he felt that the South was right—but when convinced of his error, he made haste to repair it, and when he had once taken the oath of allegiance, he went to work with all his might to aid the cause of the Union. To Mr. Langhorn is due all the honor of frustrating the designs of the *rebels from Canada*; and Col. Sweet being advised by Mr. Langhorn of *this* portion of the plot, and by the writer of the *Copperheads'* *movements and intents*, the Colonel had the best possible opportunity of acquiring important knowledge, and regulating his conduct in accordance therewith. Mr. Langhorn is a true friend of the Union, an admirer of our lamented President, and has rendered the citizens of Chicago a service which should ever be held in grateful remembrance.

MR. SHANKS—Once a Rebel officer of distinction, but now a loyal man, consistent in conduct, and of very great assistance to the Government, in ferreting out Rebel officers and Rebel sympathisers, has the confidence and respect of those who know him. He is a young man of signal ability, and if he continues to serve the country as faithfully as he has in the present case, will yet attain distinction.

CHRISTOPHER C. STRAWN—Was a valuable witness. He is a young man who has taken an active part with the Democrats, and is well informed of the incomings and outgoings, and the eccentricities and peccadillos of the managers in Chicago, although the *Post* says, that "before his arrest he was not worthy of notice, and after his arrest still less so." We think the *Post* man a little severe on Strawn, who has done all he could to have the guilty Copperhead readers of that paper brought to justice. Mr. Strawn, has bade his brethren, the Copperheads, an affectionate and, we trust, final adieu.

JOHN MAUGHAN, an Englishman, born in Berkshire county, and about 22 years of age. His family moved to Toronto, Canada West. He was always in Canada regarded as a young man, with fine business qualities and promise. For three years just before his connection with the rebels, and their Northern conspirators, he occupied a very responsible position as a clerk and teller, in one of the branches of the bank of Upper Canada, and was in every way worthy the confidence reposed in him. During the spring and summer of 1864, he however became acquainted with rebel soldiers in Canada, earnestly espoused their cause, and left his position to go with them to the Southern army. They, however, instead of going South, went to Chicago, where he became acquainted with the conspirators, and also gained their confidence, and on account of being an Englishman, and having his papers with him, and being able to travel without fear of detection, he was used by them to carry their correspondence and other communications, which were of too dangerous a character to trust to the mails. This man was truly a dangerous character. No one, except those who employed him, knew him, or the character in which he was acting, and he was able, frequently, to render the conspirators immense service in their desperate schemes. He was captured in Chicago in November, and finally agreed to turn State's evidence, when he saw that unless he did, his own life was forfeited. After this agreement, he was treated with great leniency by the Government, but upon being placed upon the witness stand, his old sympathies and prejudices returned, and it is believed he distinctly perjured himself, acting through the whole trial with bad faith toward the Government which had treated him so generously.

THOS. E. COURTNEY—A Son of Liberty, and a leading Democrat of Chicago, called a witness for *defence*, testified, among other things, as follows:

"*I was on a Committee of the Democratic party to recieve, at the Alton Depot, some bogus voters that were to be imported into Chicago to vote at the Presidential election;* they were part and parcel of the tribe that came from Egypt, and I was one of the *Committee appointed to escort them to their boarding houses.*"

OBADIAH JACKSON, JR., ESQ., Grand Seignior of the Temple, who had been arrested and sent to Camp Douglas, and while there had written and signed a "statement," was called for the defence, but it neither helped him or the defendants.

COL. B. M. ANDERSON—Was born, reared, and educated in Kentucky. He was a young man of education, ability, and fine personal appearance, and had he not been a rebel would have been an accomplished gentleman. He possessed many fine points of character, and was, in our opinion, a much better man than any of the Northern Copperheads who have been arrested. He had been in the Nicaraugua expedition, under the fillibuster, Walker. Col. Anderson was the dupe of others. He committed suicide at the barracks in Cincinnati, during the progress of the trial. He leaves a wife and many friends to mourn his death. His history is a sad one. In any other position than a rebel, he would have been a most useful member of society. He was not of the material of which the Sons of Liberty was made up, but aside from that deadly fanaticism which ruined him, he won warm friends wherever he went. Nature did everything for him, but the accursed doctrine of Calhoun, consigned him to a suicide's grave, "after life's fitful fever" of war upon the land of his birth.

CHARLES TRAVIS DANIELS—One of the prisoners, is a native of Harrison County, Ky. A lawyer by profession, about 26 years of age and very prepossessing in appearance. He is somewhat remarkable for a rather strange and singular expression of his eyes. Belonged to John H. Morgan's command, but never served in any other capacity than as an enlisted man. He was captured with Morgan during his raid in Ohio, and confined in Camp Douglas, from which he escaped; was captured at Charles Walsh's house, on the 7th of November, and escaped again from the military authorities in Cincinnati, Ohio, while being tried by the Commission. He has not been recaptured, but has been found guilty by the Commission.

CAPT. GEORGE CANTRILL—Is a native of Scott County, Ky. Is about the same age as Daniels. There is nothing remarkable in connection with him, and of no more than ordinary intelligence. He also belonged to Morgan's command, in which he served as Company commander; was in Morgan's last raid in Kentucky, and at his defeat at Cynthiana escaped to Canada. He was with the other rebels at Chicago during the Convention, and went with them to Southern Illinois for the purpose of drilling Copperheads. He was captured in the house of Charles Walsh, on the morning of the 7th of November last. On account of severe sickness he was not tried with the other conspirators.

RICHARD T. SEMMES—One of the prisoners, tried, convicted, and sentenced, for being one of the Chicago Conspirators, is a young man—not over 23 or 24 years of age, a Marylander by birth, and a lawyer by profession. He is a relation of the pirate Semmes, (unfortunate in name,) said to be a nephew. He graduated at Yale College with distinction, and his prospects in Chicago were flattering till he connected himself with the Sons of Liberty, and listened to the teachings of older and "wiser" men.

Of the witnesses for the defence we have nothing to say, further than most of them were Sons of Liberty. Some of them so far perjured themselves, that now a common lie to them is considered as good as the truth, if not a little better. It is said of Judge H. L. Burnet, that he remarked, had he known what witnesses the defence would have introduced, he would not have called any witnesses for the *Government*—they would have been superfluous. Rather severe, and we will hope he did not say it.

Space will not admit of a review of the evidence, and this will be unnecessary for all who will read the sketch of the Judge Advocate's argument.

CHAP. XXI.

ARGUMENT OF THE JUDGE ADVOCATE IN THE CONSPIRACY CASES—CONVICTION OF THE PRISONERS.

The evidence in the case before the military commission at Cincinnati, having closed, the counsel who represented the prisoners made their addresses—they cannot be called arguments—and the court adjourned to Tuesday, April 18. As lawyers who have no valid defence, observe it as a policy to attack the Government witnesses with great fury, so Messrs. Hervey and Wilson, true to the ethics of their profession, made a grand assault upon the principal witnesses. Counsellor Hervey, in his harangue, used the following language, which illustrates the line of "argument" for defence:

"Some two hundred years ago," said the learned counsel, "there was a man in England who swore away the lives of his fellow citizens by wholesale. His name was Dr. Titus Oates—the man who got up what was called the Popish plot, and by perjury and villainy, consigned many an innocent head to the scaffold. He was assisted by a man who has, as no other judge has, disgraced the ermine—Jeffries, who drank himself to death in the tower, when his co-worker in iniquities and evil deeds with dreadful and condign punishment followed him. The effort of nature to produce so great a monster was so terrible that it required a resting spell of two hundred years before she could produce another such monster in the shape of Dr. I. Winslow Ayer."

We forgive him, for he was obliged to seem to do or say something to earn his "fee." There being no arguments for defence, but only such pathetic appeals as only a lawyer, without the least hope, would make, feeling that his clients would expect *something*, we need not take our space to report their remarks.

On Tuesday April 18, Judge Advocate Burnet made his closing argument for the Government. It was truly a master-piece, complete in every part. It was such an effort as might have been expected, of one who has, during this long tedious trial, shown himself a gentleman, a profound counsellor, a true patriot and an advocate of justice, whose only aim has been to elicit truth, and be the better enabled to serve the true interests of the country. We would gladly present every argument and address he has made, during the trial, but space will not admit, and we therefore invite careful attention to the following sketch of his address:

The Judge Advocate, in referring to the accused, said:

There are two sides to this case; two sides for the manifestation of sympathy. While here is an old, white-haired man before you, whose every thing is at stake; while here is a father, a generous, open-hearted, and impulsive man, whose all is at stake; and here is a soldier, who has fought in every clime, and who has taken up his sword to destroy life in every cause, whose everything is also at stake, yet there is, on the other side, your Government at stake. If these men be guilty, justice to the nation demands of you this day that you should convict them, and you must not waver. In the consideration of this case, you must bring to your aid a power, that may be a little more than is ordinarily given to human nature. You must, for the time, sink all hatred, malice, even human sympathy; and rise, God-like, to determine the truth and adjust the punishment.

That these accused would enter upon the commission of so heinous a crime, I can scarcely permit myself to believe. They have made a strong appeal to your sympathies. Each counsel has advocated the cause of his client with an earnestness and an eloquence that does him honor; I shall always respect them, and bear them in kindly recollection.

But there seems to have been something, during these four years of the nation's trial, that has appeared to paralyze the native instincts of the American heart. This phantom, this syren of secession, with her enticing song, seems to have lulled to sleep the better part of human nature. At the sound of her voice, and the flash of her eye, men have sprung to arms, to grapple with the life of the nation, because it was free! They have followed, at the beck of the syren, over desolated homes; they have trampled over the dead corses of murdered brothers, and innocent women and children. They have blackened the land with desolation, and made it the abode of moaning and woe. She has blinded, while she has demoralized them. Old men, forgetting their white hairs, have joined in the conspiracy at the beck of this phantom, who has taken out of the human heart its heaven-born instincts, to plant there those of vengeance, and the thirst for blood.

My tongue falters as I look over this country and see bereaved widows and orphans, the white-haired patriots that mourn for the first-born, that shall ne'er greet them, and those who sit at the desolate hearth, with hands upraised, waiting for the knock that will be but the death-knell of all their hopes; and think that the phantom of secession has caused all this!

Men who were kind fathers, kind husbands and noble patriots, have forgotten it all in a day, and have become traitors, and inculcated doctrines that have, by the hands of fiends, stricken down that patriotic and noble leader of the human race. There is something in it which no man can comprehend. The doctrines which they inculcate harden the heart, and nerve the arm to crime, enabling them to commit robbery, arson and murder, for all is in her category; and as they commit those crimes, the appeal to God for the justness of their cause. That is what has deceived these men; it is this accursed phantom of secession that has blinded their eyes; that has cooled their hearts and filled them with vengeance. It is this that has changed and perverted the human instincts, that should have ruled in their breasts.

Of this man Walsh, I have simply this to say: The evidence is as you have seen it. I have briefly sketched it; I will not dwell upon much that ought to be said; I can not. The testimony is voluminous, filling 2,000 or 2,500 pages. I have had but a few days to scan through it; I have given you only the leading points, and you must judge. I would not say one word that would take from this family their father; but if this man was guilty of this crime, or has aided and abetted this conspiracy, you have but one duty to perform. You must know no man, be influenced by no bias, betray no sympathy, but must be firm in the performance of your stern duty. There are thirty millions of suffering people in this land, and against these, one man's life, if guilty, weighs little in the scale of justice. We have, unhappily, in the history of this war, frequently seen sympathy manifested for criminals, rebels and traitors—those who have brought this great injustice upon the true and the loyal. It is not mercy to acquit those guilty of cruelty to a people who are struggling for their very existence; it would be cruelty to our brave soldiers, and to those who have been left widows and orphans.

As to Judge Morris—for his white hair and old age, I have only respect. For all that is worthy in him as a citizen, I do him reverence; but if this white-haired old man has engaged in a conspiracy against my nation and my country, I turn to the other side, and see white-haired patriots who mourn in sadness because such as he have done these evil deeds,—and I remember Justice!

As to this man Grenfel, I confess I have no sympathy with him; no sympathy for the foreigner who lands in our country when this nation is engaged in the struggle for human right and human liberty, and who takes part in the quarrel against us, and arrays himself on the side of those who are trying to establish tyrany and slavery. I have no sympathy for the man whose sword is unsheathed for hire and not for principle; for whom slavery and despotism have more charms than freedom and liberty. The motive of such a one does not rise even to the dignity of vengeance. As has been said by his counsel, his sword has gleamed in every sun, and has been employed on the side of almost every nationality, and after this he engages in our struggle, and, as testified to by Colonel Moore, desires to raise the black flag against our prisoners; and after men have yielded as prisoners of war, he rides up to one, and stabs him, coward like, in the back.

But he is not true to the cause he espouses. When in Washington he went to the Secretary of War and betrays the very people with whom he had been fighting; tells all he knows of the strength, position and designs of the Confederates. He said he proposed to leave immediately for England, but he breaks his faith, proceeds to Canada, and is found among the conspirators, and is now here, charged with these crimes to-day. There is no throb of my heart that beats in unison with such conduct as this. He was a fit instrument to be used in this enterprise. What to him would be the wail of women and little ones? What to him would be the pleadings of old men and unarmed citizens?

The delivery of Judge Burnett's argument occupied three and a half hours, after which the Commission adjourned to meet at four o'clock P. M., to deliberate on the findings and sentence. They accordingly met at the hour appointed, and, after mature deliberation, finally recorded their verdict.

General Hooker issued General Orders No. 30, April 22, in which he promulgates the finding of the military commission which, for three months past, has been engaged in the trial of the alleged Chicago conspirators. The commission have acquitted Buckner S. Morris and Vincent Marmaduke, and they are to be discharged upon their taking the oath of allegiance. They find Charles Walsh and Richard T. Semmes guilty of all the charges and specifications, and sentence the former to five years' imprisonment at hard labor from the 7th of November last, and the latter to three years' imprisonment at hard labor from the same date, at such place as the commanding general may direct. Gen. Hooker has named the State penitentiary at Columbus, Ohio.

Cantrill's trial has been continued; Anderson committed suicide, and Charles Travis Daniels escaped. The commission found a verdict against Daniels, but it has not yet been promulgated. The findings against G. St. Leger Grenfell have not yet been announced officially; but it is death, at such time and place as Gen. Hooker shall designate. The commission has been dissolved.

The Chicago *Tribune*, in speaking of the sentence, says:

The trial of the Chicago conspirators has ended, the sentences have been pronounced and approved, and the court has adjourned. Buckner S. Morris and Vincent Marmaduke are acquitted and Charles Walsh and Richard T. Semmes were found guilty of the entire charges and specifications, to wit: of conspiracy for the relief of the prisoners at Camp Douglas, and of conspiring to "lay waste and destroy" the city of Chicago. Walsh is sentenced to imprisonment for five years from November 7th, 1864, and Semmes to imprisonment at hard labor for three years from the date of sentence. The findings against G. St. Leger Grenfell have not been officially promulgated, but it is stated that he is found guilty and sentenced to death, at such time and place as Gen. Hooker shall designate. The penitentiary at Columbus, Ohio, is designated as the place of confinement of Walsh and Semmes. The trial has been long, mainly by reason of the course pursued by the defense, whose aim has been to protract it, so as to tire out the perseverance of the prosecution and the patience of the court and people. The court have performed their arduous duties with great ability and fairness. The result will doubtless be satisfactory to the people. It is proved that this great crime was in all its naked deformity and depravity actually committed. It follows that the Copperhead statement, published in the rebel organ in this city, charging that the entire plot and arrest of these Copperhead traitors and assassins were invented by the Union Republicans of Chicago as an electioneering trick, was the subterfuge of conscious guilt trying to cover up its tracks and to rub out the stains of its own attempted crimes. The same organ now impugns the "competency" of the Court. It may consider itself fortunate that it has not had an opportunity to argue the question of jurisdiction on its own behalf before a similar tribunal. Its opposition to such courts originates in a feeling of uneasiness about its own safety. For

"Thief ne'er felt the halter draw
With good opinion of the law."

REV. DR. TIFFANY UPON COPPERHEADS.

At a public meeting held in Chicago, after the announcement of the assassination, Rev. Dr. Tiffany, in an able and eloquent address said:

"God alone is great. At rare intervals he sends us a man beyond the limit of our measure. Our attention has been directed to the excellences of the character which belonged to our late President, and to the spirit of the system which gave strength to the blow of the assassin. A more terrible topic is now to be discussed—our relation to that spirit—our responsibility for that blow.

We have been accustomed to say, "slavery is sectional, and freedom national." let those who elect slavery take the results of slavery to themselves; let them suffer, if their choice brings suffering; but as for us, we wash our hands in innocency, and hold ourselves guiltless of blood." And so we have been going on ever since the outbreak of slavery in the form of armed rebellion. "They are the guilty parties, let them suffer." But has all this been right? Have we had no responsibility? Is no guilt ours? We may not have owned slaves, but we may have made a common cause with men owners—may have brought condemnation upon ourselves by our tolerance, by our compromises.

Sad and almost disgraceful is the record which exhibits our complicity with this sin. We began by making free States wait at the door of the Union until slavery had a counterpoise, or balance adjusted in the form of slave State, to preserve the balance against freedom in the National Senate. We compromised the territories west of the Mississippi, by tolerating slaves there, and as one demand after another was made it was granted, till we even allowed slave rule in free States, by submitting to the Fugitive Slave law—these things could not have been done without our votes. When they threatened and blustered we fawned and cringed, until they knew and avowed their belief that the crack of a slave whip would bring the north to its knees. All they asked we granted, more than they demanded we offered. We held out our wrists for manacles. When we elected the great good man, who embodied our idea of nationality and freedom; and even after official announcement had been made of the position slavery occupied in their proposed nationalism, we guarded their slaves, and kept them secure to labor for the support of the masters who were fighting against us. When these slaves, acting on an intuition of freedom, came fleeing to us, we sent them back to chains and bondage. In all this we showed our complicity with the sin which struck the blow which killed our good President.

And after the slaughter of thousands in battle, and the death of as many more in hospitals, of fever, starvation and wounds, still was our hatred of the sin which caused them not deep enough. We talked of amnesty and non-humiliation, and God has permitted the sad cup to come to each lip in bitterness. Each one mourns to-day as if personally bereaved. The blackness of darkness is in our homes, and the whole nation mourns its first-born—its first-loved. May not—does not—a measure of responsibility rest upon us for this last sad event? Have we not been tolerant of the treason which has wrought this crime? Have we not been apologists for infamy under the name of different political opinions? Have we not spared when we should have punished—been merciful when mercy was but cruelty? We seem to have believed that because there were more serpents away from our homes, the few left here had no venom. We felt secure because the loyalists were more numerous than the traitors. But of the few who were here, and tolerated here, some plotted the escape of rebel prisoners, some the burning of our city, some the conflagration of New York, and some the murder of the Cabinet, while one has killed the good President. Had they all been driven out, or put under strict surveillance, there would have been none of these things from them. We have lost our President by tolerating traitors in our streets.

Who was the assassin of the President? Not an armed rebel, clothed with belligerent rights; not a political refugee, who had skulked into our lines for rapine and for plunder; but the citizen of a free State, who could visit and send his cards to the Vice-President with a flippant familiarity, which his aristocratic slave-holding associates presume to use,—a man allowed to go about the streets of Washington, breathing treason and blaspheming God, without rebuke. He could command attention from proprietors of houses and saloons, from owners of blooded stock, from men who were called loyal, and the toleration of this killed our good President.

He was a wretch, of whom a press said, but yesterday, that he was sincere in thinking he should rid the earth of a tyrant, by slaying the President, this sincerity must place him on a level with John Brown. [Hisses and cries of *The Times*.] This was said yesterday, and read by thousands, and I know of no steps taken to prevent the utterance of similar insult and outrage to-morrow. For this tolerance we are responsible, and tolerance like this killed the good President. When a far-seeing military commandant ordered the suppression of published treason, there were men in high places, and men all over the land, who outraged the loyal masses by interfering to prevent the execution of that order, on the ground of disturbing the freedom of the press; but when our ministers went into Richmond they were muzzled, and the result has been that treason has been uttered, the good man called an *imbecile*—the generous man a *tyrant*—the restraint of traitors has has been referred to as, *usurpation* of power, and prisons have been called *Bastiles*. All this has been, and we have tolerated it. This has given aid and comfort to treason in the South, and traitors in the North, and this has killed the good President.

The measure of our responsibility is the amount of our connivance at these things. No man is free from guilt who has winked at this wrong, who has interfered to prevent the punishment of wrong-doers, who has apologies for treason, who has not done all in his power to rebuke, denounce and punish the foes of the nation, at home and abroad. We stand, to-day, as though in the presence of the nation's dead, and here, on the tomb of our chieftain, let us swear eternal enmity to treason and to traitors. Nor let us, when the assassin shall be arrested and punished—oh! let us not then think we have done our duty. I had rather the profane wretch who has done this deed were never taken, than that his execution should relieve our minds from one thought of our personal responsibility. No; rather let the wretch be a fugitive and vagabond, with the mark of Cain upon him. Let none slay him, for we ourselves are not guiltless. And as he flies from men, with hate in his eyes and hell in his heart, let every home be an asylum from which he shall be barred, and every honest, loyal heart a sanctuary where no thought of complicity with him, or sympathy for him may enter. Let us bow before God to-day in humble penitence; let us ask of Him forgiveness—Father forgive us, for we knew not what we did—that His hand be stayed, and the measure of our responsibility be canceled.

In this connection, we may with propriety, introduce the following extract from President Johnson's recent speech to the Indiana delegation :

"We are living at a time when the public mind had almost become oblivious of what treason is. The time has arrived, my countrymen, when the American people should be educated and taught what crime is, and that treason is crime, and the highest crime known to the law and the Constitution. Yes, treason against a State, treason against all the States, treason against the Government of the United States, is the highest crime that can be committed, and those engaged in it should suffer all the penalties. It is not promulgating anything that I have not heretofore said, to say that traitors must be made odious; that treason must be made odious; that traitors must be punished and imprisoned. [Applause.] They must not only be punished, but their social power must be destroyed. If not, they will still maintain an ascendency, and may again become numerous and powerful; for, in the words of a former senator of the United States, when traitors become numerous enough, treason becomes respectable. And I say that, after making treason odious, every

Union man and the Government, should be renumerated out of the pockets of those who have inflicted the great suffering upon the country. [Applause.] But do not understand me as saying this in a spirit of anger; for, if I understand my own heart, the reverse is the case; and, while I say that the penalties of the law, in a stern and inflexible manner, should be executed upon conscious, intelligent, and influential traitors,—the leaders who have deceived thousands upon thousands of laboring men, who have been drawn into the rebellion; and while I say, as to leaders, punishment, I also say leniency, conciliation, and amnesty, to the thousands whom they have misled and deceived, and, in relation to this, as I have remarked, I might have adopted your speech as my own."

LIST OF PROMINENT MEMBERS OF THE "SONS OF LIBERTY" IN ILLINOIS.

List of names of prominent members of the "Sons of Liberty" in the several counties of the State of Illinois, as reported by Col. J. B. Sweet.

Names.	County.	Name.	County.
James W. Singleton	Adams.	M. Simmons	Jo Davies.
Thomas P. Bond	Bond.	Louis Shisler	Jo Davies.
Harry Wilton	Bond.	Thomas McKee	Knox.
Thos. Hunter	Bond.	J. F. Worrell	McLean.
Martin Brooks	Brown	E. D. Wright	Menard.
C. H. Atwood	Brown.	Edward Lanning	Menard.
Fred Reavick	Cass.	Robert Halloway	Mercer.
Allen J. Hill	Cass.	Robert Davis	Montgomery.
David Epler	Cass.	Thomas Grey	Montgomery.
James A. Dick	Cass.	W. J. Latham	Morgan.
Samuel Christey	Cass.	J. O. S. Hays	Morgan.
T. J. Clark	Champaigne.	J. W. McMillen	Morgan.
James Morrow	Champaigne.	D. Patterson	Moultrie.
H. M. Vandeveer	Christian.	Dr. Kellar	Moultrie.
J. H. Clark	Christian.	G. D. Read	Ogle.
S. S. Whitehed	Clark.	W. W. O'Brien	Peoria.
H. H. Peyton	Clark.	Peter Sweat	Peoria.
Phillip Dougherty	Clark.	Jacob Gale	Peoria.
A. M. Christi n	Clay.	P. W. Dunue	Peoria.
Stephen B. Moore	Coles.	John Fuller	Peoria.
Dr. Wickersham	Cook.	John Francis	Peoria.
G. S. Kimberly	Cook.	C. H. Wright	Peoria.
S. Corning Judd	Fulton.	John Oug	Putnam.
Charles Sweeny	Fulton.	M. Richard..on	Shelby.
L. Walker	Hamilton.	M. Shallenberger	Stark.
M. Couchman	Hancock.	J. B. Smith	Stevenson.
M. M. Morrow	Hancock.	J. L. Carr	Vermillion.
J. M. Finch	Hancock.	John Donlar	Vermillion.
Dennis Smith	Hancock.	Wm. S. Moore	Christian.
J. S. Rainsdell	Henderson.	B. S. Morris	Cook.
A. Johnson	Henderson.	W. C. Wilson	Crawford.
Ira R. Wills	Henry.	L. W. Onell	Crawford.
Chas. Durham	Henry.	Dickins	Cumberland.
Morrison Francis	Henry.	J. C. Armstrong	Dewitt.
J. D. Carpenter	Henry.	C. H. Palmer	Dewitt.
J. Osborn	Jackson.	B. T. Williams	Douglas.
G. W. Jeffries	Jasper.	Amos Green	Edgar.
G. H. Varnell	Jefferson.	R. M. Bishop	Edgar.
Wm. Dodds	Jefferson.	W. D. Latshaw	Edwards.
J. M. Pace	Jefferson.	Levi Eckels	Fayette.
James Sample	Jersey.	Dr. Bassett	Fayette.
O. W. Powell	Jersey.	T. Greathouse	Fayette.
M. Y. Johnson	Jo Davies.	Chas. T. Smith	Fayette.
David Shean	Jo Davies.	N. Simmons	Ford.

Names.	County.	Names.	County.
Ed. Gill	Ford.	R. Caswell	McLean.
A. D. Duff	Franklin.	J. C. Springer	McLean.
B. F. Pope	Franklin.	T. Alexander	Putnam.
W. B. Kelly	Franklin.	W. H. G. Burney	Putnam.
A. Perry	Fulton.	H. B. Kays	Putnam.
J. H. Peilsob	Fulton.	E. S. Wilson	Richmond.
E. D. Helm	Knox.	J. W. Barrott	Sangamon.
J. M. Nicholson	Knox.	W. T. Barrett	Sangamon.
James Dethridge	Knox.	Jacob Epier	Sangamon.
E. Elsworth	Knox.	B. B. Piper	Sangamon.
D. H. Morgan	Lawrence.	W. M. Springer	Sangamon.
E. D. Norton	Logan.	E. Edmonston	Schuyler.
A. M. Miller	Logan.	P. L. Campbell	Schuyler.
R. J. Housy	Macoupin.	J. Montgomery	Schuyler.
Dr. T. M. Hope	Madison.	J. C. Fox	Schuyler.
H K. S. O'Melveny	Marion.	J. N. Ward	Schuyler.
S. R. Carigan	Marion.	G. W. Mentz	Schuyler.
John Burns	Marshall.	F. B. Thompson	Shelby.
P. M, Janney	Marshall.	Rueben Ruessler	Shelby.
C. M. Baker	Marshall.	W. Friend	Wabash.
R. Smithson	Marshall.	C. Z. Landes	Wabash.
J. R. Teggart	Marshall.	S. B. McCourtney	Warren.
J. Haringhorst	Mason.	N. K. Poeffer	Warren.
J. S. Chamberlain	Mason.	John Hanus	Warren.
J. W. Mathews	McDon'h.	G. W. Aiken	Williamson.
J. C. Thompson	McDon'h.	R. M. Hendley	Williamson.
Thomas A. Musteve	McDon'h.	C. A. Richardson	Woodford.
Wm. H. Neece	McDon'h.		

www.ingramcontent.com/pod-product-compliance
Lightning Source LLC
Chambersburg PA
CBHW021944160426
43195CB00011B/1217